MW01092141

A FLOWER FOR GOD

For permission requests, contact wilsondukedba@gmail.com.

Printed in the United States of America:
First Printing, 2021
Spiritual Memoir
ISBN 978-0-9985386-7-9

Prema J. Camp photo by Megan Sciera
Book Design by Megan Sciera and Scout James

All quotes by Meher Baba copyright © Avatar
Meher Baba Perpetual Public Charitable Trust.
Visit @ www.avatarmeherbabatrust.org
Meher Baba photo copyright © Meher Nazar
Publications used by permission.
All quotes in this book cited from *A Course in Miracles* © are from the 3rd edition. Foundation for Inner Peace, P.O. Box 598, Mill Valley, CA 94942-0598, www.acim.org and info@acim.org

Wilson Duke Press
Seattle, WA

A FLOWER FOR GOD

PREMA JASMINE CAMP
A MEMOIR

A FLOWER FOR GOD

"An inspiring and inspired life story of a delicate yet strong soul in search of the Real Self. A journey through the inevitable suffering of a seeker—loss, love, and determination. What a treasure!"
— *Valeria Violati, a friend in Italy*

"Your descriptions transport the reader to your grandparents' farm. It is beautiful there; it's an awakening to another time."
— *Willene Johnson, Artist*

"Your writing, endearingly intimate and disarmingly honest, gives the reader a vicarious feeling of being a part of the setting. Your poignant thoughts, which are a function of your rich inner and outer experiences, stir emotions and tend to make one introspective."
— *Amitabh Mukherjee, Software Professional*

"You transport me to the time and the space not only as yourself but as a quiet, yet intimate onlooker."
— *Cynthia Johnson, MSW in Massachusetts*

"I appreciate your enthusiastic dedication to each love of your life. Even the events of your life that are shared with such zeal seem rare and fascinating to me."
—*Theresa Wesly, Co-Minister of Spirit of Truth Church*

"Very clear, lucid, and tasty writing."

— *Bob Petrucci, Childhood Classmate*

"You see things from a whole different perspective and then assimilate them into your life. I would love to see the world through your eyes."

— *Leslie Haswell, Family Law Attorney*

"I was at times transported into that exhilarating world of the mind that lifts us out of our mundane concerns and affirms what is important and of real value in life."

— *Rose Reed, author of Journey in Consciousness*

"I particularly applaud the honesty and love in 'To an Angry Daughter.'"

— *Caroline O'Hagan, Meherabad resident*

"'God is in the details' rings true for me about this memoir. Prema's ability to transport one through her poems and nuanced prose almost reads like a piece of fiction; this is a journey of a well-crafted character with true transformation. Stunning!"

— *Preeti Hay, Freelance Writer*

"Reads like a diary that is characterized by a tendency to find good in everything."

— *Scott Cramer, author of The Toucan Trilogy*

"I think your book is delightful!!! Love your unique style."

— *Mary Lloyd, Energy healing*

"With all the books stacked up to read, I couldn't resist yours.
Once started it was mesmerizing. Your descriptions of your life
in India are so simple, so down-to-earth, beautiful and humble."

— Joan Quay, remembered as a very special soul, a seeker
of beauty

"The chapter 'Early Occult Experiences' is a delicate read, very
much like its author! Your prose reflects well your being. Interesting, smooth flow like a river just large enough to make no mur-
murs. Gentle."

— Eric Solibakke, Meherabad resident

Dedication

To my parents, who shared their love of surrounding nature
that I inherited and who I recognized as my spiritual teachers
when writing this book.

TABLE OF CONTENTS

Poetry & Song

Acknowledgments

My first and most important thank you is to Meher Baba, who is the One who gave the inner message to write. Within hours, I had a first chapter. My heartfelt thanks go to Cynthia Johnson and Amitabh (Titu) Mukherjee, pilgrims who each gave me an invaluable suggestion that I followed. My thanks also go to a certain group of ladies staying at the Meher Pilgrim Center. I remember all of you telling me that you wanted to read more. Thank you, ladies, for confirming that my young story needed to continue.

I offer my enduring gratefulness to the late Pat Schneider, who mentored me through years of workshops and always took the time to email words of encouragement, answering each of my questions. Pat is my quintessential role model for truth-telling in writing. To my husband then, Paul Sherburne, thank you for your nights of putting our two-year-old to bed and seeing that her sister went to bed on time so that I could go to writing workshops; you were in the vanguard of my supporters. To my earliest editor, Anna Kirwan, thank you for words that brought my feelings into a lyrical form, as you defined my book as a memoir (I hadn't known) and called it "spiritually intensely moving." Abundant thanks to Rosie Pearson, now editor, for eight years of companionable accomplishment as you've taught as well as edited.

To my daughter Megan Sciera, who is the book's designer and cover artist, thank you for knowing since age eight that I am a writer. Thank you also to my daughter, Beth Russell, who at age seven wrote her first poem and inspired me to write my first as well. And as a poet, I thank another Beth, Beth Clifford, for the perfect gem of her poetic words that evoke this book. Beyond this, my appreciation extends to all those unnamed here who have given me just the boost of help or confidence I needed. You have your place in my gratitude.

Foreword

Not coincidentally, I met Prema at a Spiritual Journaling workshop. Although there were only three of us, including Prema, I left her home that afternoon with a connection to her writing and an appreciation of her gentle, specific feedback on mine.

I moved to Springfield, Massachusetts from Boston at the end of 1989 to take a job as an IT Project Manager. Finding a writing group was a priority only slightly less urgent than locating the grocery store in my new neighborhood. Oddly enough, I found the writing group in the grocery store, or rather on its busy bulletin board, which hung on a wall between two sets of automatic doors. Stopping to read the board risked creating a pileup that might require management intervention. Each time I left the checkout, I slowed my progress toward the exit and waited for a lull in the traffic to scan the board to find ways to amuse myself until I made some friends in my new hometown.

One day in 1992, I found a poster printed on construction paper inviting writers to join a workshop in Longmeadow. I ripped off one of the fringe pieces containing a phone number and called as soon as I got home. The answering machine took my request for a call back on either my home or work phone.

A few days later, I received a call at work.

"My daughter's name is Beth," she said and murmured something about that being a good sign. I wasn't sure I agreed.

I asked about the requirements for membership in this group. Assuring me there were none, Prema launched into a description of her method of facilitating and took several digressionary paths away and back into the subject of this group. She asked if I'd like to attend a workshop the following Saturday on Spiritual Journaling. Taken aback, since she had, at a previous turn, mentioned that the group met on Wednesday nights, I said "Ok," and jotted down the address.

My fears of walking into a den of tea leaf reading nuts were allayed immediately. Prema got down to business at the appointed time, having shown me and the other participant where to hang our coats and find the bathroom. Her facilitation was specific and consistent. If we strayed from any rule she had announced at the outset, she quickly reminded us of the rule and its purpose, while encouraging us to go on. Prema urged me to claim the title of writer. As a result of her feedback and support, now retired, I pursued an MFA in Creative Nonfiction at Bay Path University in Longmeadow, Massachusetts, which I received in the spring of 2020.

That was the beginning of my friendship with Prema, a friendship that was also a mentorship in trusting the process and letting the pen just move across the page. *A Flower for God* illustrates Prema's lifelong trust in a process that allowed her to move through anger and grief to a place of peace.

A spiritual journey is just that, a journey. It's a long trek through mortal experiences that teach us, humble us, and make us long for deliverance from our human failings. The first stop on this journey is often awareness. Prema describes her first memory of awareness at the age of seven in the loft of her grandparents' barn:

> *Lying on a bale, I watched swallows swoop in and out, hearing their wings beat softly and the hay whispering against the worn paint of the open door. Mostly, no voices carried from the house. What thoughts I had came and went like the swallows. I drifted in daydreams, feeling still and empty and without words. In my child's vocabulary I didn't know what a sanctuary was—nor the meaning of meditation. I didn't know I had a soul. But I knew I could feel that my body wasn't there without any words about it. I was more wind than child.*

What a paradox that her early recognition of a world without words brought her to self-exploration through language. Her poetry uses words to penetrate the unexplainable. Her prose invites intimacy by sharing experiences she can't know we share. Her courage is to tell us anyway. She writes to her daughter

Forgive me

> *...for standing close and telling you not to leave. What I meant was, never leave, stay weak as egg white, simple as jelly, young as a pullet, ineffectual as dough. I got out the umbilical cord and in seconds tried to tie us together again.*

Vulnerability is what laid her bare and made her strong. The spiritual journey is always one of pain. Without it, there would be no reason to seek relief. During her journey, Prema succumbed to pain and rose to recovery not once but repeatedly. Each cycle yielded an epiphany and more openness to divine manifestations. While confined in a psychiatric ward, she experienced such a sign.

> *... one day while showering, I saw sudden, blinding flashes of light, something that had happened to me once before when I was in junior high, but this time they brought me to my knees. Crawling to my bed I rang the bell. The doctor said it was a drug reaction, but without knowing what had happened, I knew that he was wrong.... I left the hospital facing the fact that I had a relationship addiction that was codependency, and only years later would I recognize that the flashes had had a spiritual meaning.*

Prema's internal compass told her, despite expert opinion and her own fears, that her experience was not explainable in any human way. Her faith in the reality of spiritual signals in everyday life made it possible for her to find hope along her journey.

She became open to manifestations of the divine that eluded others. By following the internal guidance that is the divine within us all, Prema found human navigators for her arrival at each stage of her spiritual journey. Her message does not proselytize the destination she chose but encourages others to embark on their own quests for solace.

Beth Clifford, Springfield, Massachusetts
June 2020

Preface

In its earliest stages of writing, *A FLOWER FOR GOD* was born the third week of September 2003, in Samadhi, the Tomb-Shrine of Avatar Meher Baba at Meherabad, near Arangaon Village and the city of Ahmednagar, in Maharashtra, a state of western India. Following an inner voice to leave and begin writing, an obsession began that lasted five months, until the writing stopped as suddenly as it had started. For two and a half years the pages remained untouched. Then, in September 2006, a second message came. It was time to return to writing.

These chapters are memories of my spiritual awakening and journey with God long before I was aware of God as present in my life. What had been undefined and unresolved in childhood erupted in my thirties. At forty-seven, my spiritual nature appeared, to leave me at an abyss at fifty-four. Then, trusting my spiritual teacher, I made a leap of faith toward real love.

Prema Jasmine Camp
April 2021
Meherabad

Introduction

WELCOME.

Before you begin reading *A FLOWER FOR GOD*, I'd like you to know about Meher Baba as the one I know of as God. He is my best friend. (When I first met Him in inner voice, in August 1997, I called Him "my best bud"—because that was how I felt treated.) I ask for His guidance, He gives it to me, and I listen. I cherish His kindness and His comfort. Each morning I tell Him that I love Him and thank Him for awakening more of His love in my heart. Anywhere I am in the world, I feel Meher Baba's presence, helping me to change my life from one with views that disrupt my world to one with new buds of real love opening in me.

One name has been changed for privacy.

Amid chatter
A small voice speaks
Listen inward

PJC 2010

GROWING

CHAPTER I

The Hayloft

1952

Barns awaken our senses. They...can shelter
more than mere hay and animals. They can be
playgrounds for the soul.... You can escape
in a barn.[1]

Don Perkins

Summers in the 50s, before my brother was born, my sister and I went to North Newport, Maine for a week with our grandparents. I remember my happy relief at the first view of the barn and farmhouse after riding for eight hours. It was at that point in our trip that my father turned off the county road onto the gravel driveway at the mailbox with L.W. Titcomb on the post. Slowly, the Plymouth drove by the flagpole and the bed with red and blue flowers in rows, and then stopped at the barn doors and impatiently we were out.

Grammie came down the steps and across the yard smiling and then hugging. Her eyes twinkled as she said, "There's doughnuts!" And in a minute I was in the kitchen. My fingers sticky. My teeth pulling open the warm, brown crust. My mouth watering with sweetness.

Hayfields that grew out to the road surrounded the farm, hugging the buildings, except out front, where the grass was cut so short it looked as if it had been ironed. There were no trees and in the bright sun the farmhouse shone like white boiled icing. A thick mat of green vines rolled down for summer hung over the screened porch. The windows sparkled.

Those summers—I remember the distant voices from other rooms. Hay in a breeze that rustled against boards. And stillness. I felt quiet and alone, but boredom didn't quite happen because there were sheds and an attic and doors to the fields. Then woods.

Made to nap every day after the noon meal, my sister and I would lie on our beds, her small, white wrought iron against the window and my double headboard tight against a corner safe that was big and black with gold lettering. I kept quiet, not napping but looking at a whole wall of family pictures. In this room, my mother's old room, there was barely enough distance to get by between the beds, but older, I would come to understand the far greater distance that separated the farm from our home in a suburb. There, my mother loved her spacious, east-to-west bedroom, with a large, graceful tree just beyond an upper porch where she could suntan. Yet because she had grown up in this bedroom, I was able to do some of my growing up in this room too.

However not for forty-five years, and in a place far from this one, would I know of the unavoidable necessity and have the courage to face emotionally growing from a girl into a woman.

My grandmother was Grammie, plump around the middle, wearing a bib-apron over her housedress, her light gray hair a cap that rolled into a curl to softly frame her face, her narrow feet laced into black shoes with sturdy heels for support, and gold, rimless glasses that she put on with trembling fingers while she asked us, "What have you young'uns been up to?" Now I see her as not ever needing the compliments she received—an unpretentious, talented lady who had taught in a one-room school, cooked for the hired man and teacher who boarded, and had a feeling for flowers and food and a clean farm—a woman who made an elegance of simple, country living.

From the time that he was a young man, my grandfather had had a meat wagon; I've seen my mother's photo of him standing beside it. The family ate well then and later, when he became a meat inspector for the state of Maine. But with us he was Grampa, who surprised us by putting a saddle on the barn's low swing, tightening the straps as we waited excitedly.

For many years, I imagined the farm of my mother's time, not through my mother's eyes but through mine—my grandmother harnessing the pony to the cart and taking my mother for a ride or tucking a robe over her in the sleigh before Beauty's hoofs broke snow on the road to church. The tin in the kitchen was full of homemade cookies (yet later I learned that through my mother's eyes, as a child, a store-bought cookie had been a treat). The meat came from the cows my grandfather butchered in the barn. In time I saw the truth—that life was hard.

In the kitchen I listened to talk of who was driving by, and how fast they were going. A door in one corner opened to steep, narrow stairs to the cellar where Grammie sent me for jars of green beans and cucumber relish. Staring into the damp, dark air, I crept down, each foot feeling for the next step until light from the open door made the glass gleam softly in rows of narrow boards on the stone wall. When she needed potatoes, I got on my knees outside the crawl hole, then gingerly reached into the hill and counted the right number of small, hard potatoes, grasping them one at a time. When she needed beans, I'd go through the L-shape sheds that connected the kitchen to the barn, to a small, dusty-windowed room where a tall sack of white kidney beans leaned against the wall. They'd rattle in the tin cup as I walked. She'd wash them on Friday to start the soaking for Saturday's baked beans. All day I smelled the sweet, dark molasses aroma swelling in the bean pot, escaping into the kitchen.

From my seat at the dining room table, I could see the wooden posts of drying lines out back (where in grass up to my thighs I hung clothes), the corner cabinet where I got the dish of soft butter and tumblers that I filled with refrigerated water, and beyond either side of the desk, the green wall of leaves around the porch. Behind me, the curved buffet held the wedding dishes. I pressed my waist against the big, round, linen-covered table and through clouds of steam, watched everyone talking and helping themselves to heaps of mashed potatoes and glistening vegetables in china bowls, forking overlapped slices of pot roast from the platter and ladling brown-speckled gravy on top... then taking soft bread from the stack. Hungry before dinner from smelling the cooking, I filled my plate, with its rim of roses. At home, we didn't have vinegar and sugar for lettuce, but at the farm we did. We ate fresh peas too, but not like here where I heard my aunt and uncle made a meal, in season, of only peas, salt, and butter. After the main meal, there was pie or maybe ginger cookies that I broke just to hear them snap.

The barn stood at the end of the driveway, built of rough wood inside and painted white on the outside. Big doors opened to a cathedral-height expanse above and wide, uneven, splintery floorboards below where my grandparents' black Ford sat parked. On the back wall, a paned window had a dusty view to the fields, and high overhead were two long rows of old license plates nailed edge to edge. I'd stand, just looking and wondering where they'd all come from. The workroom had tools in homes of nails pounded in around their shapes and a workbench where we watched Grampa skin the hornpout we caught. Then we'd take it to Grammie for the flouring and the frying.

Stalls, unused for years, had smells for my nose and my imagination. I'd stand inside them in air that was barely moving in the heat of the barn, even with the big front and back doors rolled back. In the stillness, I'd breathe in the reminders of animals, pretending that I could hear the cows and horses stomping and chewing.

In the biggest room for hay, I climbed a ladder propped against the wall to the loft. From up there, through that large, open back door, the sunny field looked like a framed picture. I felt different in the hayloft. Lying on a bale, I watched swallows swoop in and out, hearing their wings beat softly and the hay whispering against the worn paint of the open door. Mostly, no voices carried from the house. What thoughts I had came and went like the swallows. I drifted in daydreams, feeling still and empty and without words. In my child's vocabulary I didn't know what a sanctuary was—or the meaning of meditation. I didn't know I had a soul. But I knew I could feel that my body wasn't there without any words about it. I was more wind than child.

I stayed until my grandmother's voice searched out my disappearance. "Yoo hoo, Barbara," she called in four soprano notes. I was farther away than I knew or she guessed, as her voice carried across the yard and echoed, hollow and distant, through the barn from where she stood by the opened shed door. It was my name, yet it was not who I was in those moments.

My mother married a man who had grown up in apartments in Brooklyn, and he would come to love the farm in a way that she could not. When she moved to Massachusetts, she discovered she preferred the ocean and sandy beaches to fields. It would be my father who I felt close to at the farm. But I grew up to love both beach and country. I regretted that my daughters would never rush out of the car at the barn and eat warm doughnuts, yet for them it might not have been what it was for me, in my innocence—a silent opening to the unfathomable world of God.

GLADYS BUSWELL TITCOMB

Grandmother, you were steel once
under milk-white skin. In waves
of sun your hair hung
to your waist.

Your hands seeded beans
in straight, long rows and freed
crisp, embroidered pillowslips
from the wind's fist.

Children circled you, flower-like,
Rowena, wild brown-eyed daisy, born in July;
Charles, on Christmas night,
a winter violet opening in north light.

You wished your hair weren't thin;
it was fine as talcum.
You marked Bible verses with ribbon,
grosgrain ironed by your thumb.

Geraniums, red-hot cinnamons,
bloomed inside the farm kitchen window.
"What would the neighbors say?" you worried
as you swept dust out the back shed door.

PJC   1984

CHAPTER 2

Yard and Home

1948–1955

Everyone has moments of happiness,
glimpses of truth, fleeting experiences
of affinity with God; what everyone
longs for is to make them permanent.[1]

Meher Baba

As a child, when I felt alone and adrift, I found comfort and safety in my yard—a handful of lilac held to my nose, listening to birds hidden by trees, summer grass soft under my feet, then the leaves turning red, yellow, brown and raking them for burning in a fire. What I remember from the period through elementary school is less about people and more about my yard and home. Looking back, I have become aware that those memories made from childhood experiences could be what held me together through the turmoil of emotions that was slipping into my writing by the time I reached my mid-thirties, hidden in metaphor, as yet unclear in meaning and irretrievable on paper, until my mid-forties, when I reached a watershed—to become emotionally healthy or flounder forever without my own safe space of being. Now I know that God was in those moments, still held in my mind from my childhood.

I remember

> ...on one side of the brick walk leading to our white colonial home, a tilting, blue spruce tree, and on the other, a wide copper beech with a ladder of branches where, scared and brave, I climbed higher than my bedroom window. Straddled on a branch, not moving, I bent my head to watch clouds. When my mother called, I didn't answer.

I remember

...thick, mowed grass sloping to a profusion of flowers
in a long bed, then a three-board fence where the garden began with its cucumber and squash vines, rows
of radish and carrot tops, lettuce, stakes with pole
beans and tomatoes, firm shoots of asparagus that
I weeded, and the raspberry patch where I picked
berries until my bare arms were reddened by prickles.
Farthest from the house was the stone wall with the
stone pile at one end and at the other, bittersweet's
small red berries inside split yellow jackets, with a
sour cherry tree and the peak of the compost pile
full of fat worms nearby. Hidden by vines, I kept my
balance, stepping from stone to stone, popping the
pale green insides of tough-skinned grapes into my
open mouth.

I remember

...on late summer afternoons, sitting far away from
the house with my legs grass-cooled after a hot day,
hunting for four-leaf clovers I easily found—a girl
who would read for hours on her bed with the door
closed. Alone within myself, I was unaware that God
was there, a hidden, constant companion.

I remember

...a home of uncluttered simplicity, a living room with
its polished wood furniture and attractive, uphol-
stered chairs on narrow, maple floorboards, where
looking through a window, I remembered the bush's
name—andromeda.

...climbing the narrow stairs to the attic and kneeling at the small dormer window of the finished room, finding the backyard miniature, and me, small and far away.

...opening the green door to the basement where I hung laundry in the furnace room or balanced by my waist on the opened freezer, afraid I would fall into the frigid air while reaching for a box of peas.

I remember

...rhododendrons beyond the bay window, under which oak leaves, mulched in September, disappeared under snow by early December. The rhododendrons, with their curled, dark-green leaves in crystal coats, hunkered down until April, when then freed, dripped like rain.

I remember

...in winter, paper caps frozen atop bottles delivered by the Hood's milkman, while in the kitchen, the green radiator hissed, melting snow on boots ... then spring pussy willows cut from a roadside swamp lay on the floor, as a big, curved-glass pitcher was filled with tepid water.

I remember

...listening in the night for the grandfather clock that chimed every fifteen minutes and bonged on the hour in the dining room.

I remember

...the living room, with its oval, confetti-colored,
hand-braided rug between the sofa and fireplace,
and the French doors that opened to a room that
wasn't a room, but an airy, fine meshed porch where I
could view east, south, and west. I rocked on an old,
squeaking glider, watching the robins, nesting in the
euonymus trees, bring worms to their babies. Lulled
into feeling free of the earth, I balanced in a place
where time stopped.
Or slept.

1952
AUGUST

Maple leaves wilt
to plastic wrap
in the tent of heat
pitched over the day.

Hidden cicadas buzz
like the back doorbell
under the thumb
of a neighbor's child.

Beneath a tree-umbrella,
a girl rides a raft
of roots, dirt-cool,
idly rubbing the bark.

PJC 1982

1954

CANASTA

Every day of summer after fifth grade,
Jane and I play canasta.
She shuffles two decks,
bends the pack into a pyramid
so the cards drop with the whirr-r
of a fan until the last card
lands, then pushes them
into one stack. I cut.
She deals. We sit on the asparagus-
green living room carpet. I see
blond piano legs, magazines
and an ashtray on the coffee table,
the sofa's blue-on-white colonial
slipcover, and the bottom three drawers
of a polished dresser in the hall.

Her mother serves pea soup.
It's thick and tastes funny.
She makes red-flannel hash.
I ask what's in it—"roast beef
and beets." I take four
homemade oatmeal cookies.
Jane's house is bigger than mine;
we do what we want.

When we play hide and seek,
we flatten ourselves under beds
and climb up the garage roof
until her mother tells us
to get down. This summer

I imagine I am rich like Jane,
with a closet full of clothes
and Capezio flats—all the best
colors in the rainbow.

I'm pretty good at canasta, but Jane
mostly wins because her parents
play bridge and mine don't.
I hide outside the dining room,
eavesdropping while Jane eats
Sunday dinner so we can continue.

Her father makes her excuse herself
before leaving the table.
We don't play much at my home.
It's big but not comfortable
for kids, which I can't explain.

We keep making canastas that summer
and get through—innocent and good
as the fifties makes us.

PJC   1982

CHAPTER 3

Gospel Tents and the Unitarian Church

1949–1991

The next best approach for the understanding
of the spirit is through the heart and not
through the mind.[1]

Meher Baba

My parents had different views of religion that I took on. I was less aware of my mother's influence, as hers was in the home, and more aware of my father's as he played an active role in the church we went to. In time I learned that each had a spiritual truth for me that I hadn't understood until years after its being spoken. Even further along, I realized that they were probably unaware at the time of the true meaning of their words and could not have explained the significance even to themselves. I believe their messages to me were coming through them but not from them.

I grew up in the small, simply furnished Unitarian Church in Reading, Massachusetts, my hometown, located about 50 miles from Boston. The church had stone walls softened by ivy and a bell whose chime reached my bedroom on Sunday mornings. Although my mother went to church, she was less regular about attending. She preferred to stay at home. And so it was my father who took my sister and me. When we came through the front door after the short walk back, my mother had the dining room table set with china and goblets. My church memories mingle with the aroma of roast beef waiting with twice-baked potatoes, yellow wax beans, green olives, and thick slices of beefsteak tomatoes. Then the tart and warmed rhubarb pie appeared with vanilla ice cream melting to a sweet puddle before I finished. My mother was her own church. Soon after doing the nighttime dishes, she went up to her bedroom to fall asleep at an early hour after repeating the Twenty-third Psalm and the Lord's Prayer by herself.

The year I was in third grade, my mother taught Sunday school and brought green beans for us to grow in tin cans filled with dirt. I don't remember at what age I began saying the bedtime prayer she taught me, only its gentle rhythm before falling asleep.

> Now I lay me down to sleep,
> I pray the Lord my soul to keep.

If I should die before I wake,
I pray the Lord my soul to take.

As I repeated it without understanding what all of the words meant, its rhythm comforted me as I looked away from the bedroom's shadowy corners. When I first learned in spiritual study that I was a soul that did, in truth, return to God each night and reawaken to the world each morning, I would remember the little prayer and wonder at the presence of God, and my child's voice having repeated this truth a thousand times.

My mother had a lovely voice that rose enthusiastically when she told us about riding with her parents at night past the gospel tents and hearing singing pour out into the darkness. She'd swing her right arm, snapping her fingers, and slide her feet several steps in rhythm to the memory. I would imagine something mysteriously exciting going on inside those tents that captured her imagination; yet beyond appearing to the side of the headlights, the view remained unknown, disappearing into the remainder of my memory.

Tucked away in my mind, her words reappeared when I was forty-eight. A friend named Stephen invited me to go to his church, where I entered a world unknown to me until that morning. Scarcely had the congregation begun the opening song when I knew an instant bond with my mother as the spark of rising gospel voices that had ignited her heart now lit mine. I joined in, exuberantly picking up verses, and sang thirty-five rounds of "This Little Light of Mine," feeling joyful. Without turning my face from the minister, I leaned my shoulder against Stephen's, my smile so wide my mouth could hardly form the words, and told him, "I've come home."

It was my father, raised as a Lutheran, who decided that our family would go to a Unitarian Church where we could form our own beliefs. When he occasionally spoke of going to his child-hood church, he might launch into the first half-dozen lines of the Apostles' Creed as his way of showing us what he didn't want for us. Over the following years, after moving away from home, I would find the church of my childhood in other states, feeling comfortable with the sermons and slender ritual, yet never com-mitted to becoming a member. When approaching fifty, I began exploring spirituality as different from religion, and I felt grateful to my father for my having no tether of beliefs to break.

In that small church in Reading, and from my mother's bed-time prayers, years later when I first heard an inner voice speak its gentle message of encouragement to me, it came from the Twen-ty-third Psalm, familiar and comforting.

It took longer still to experience the insight into the gifts of words my parents gave me in later years. Visiting my parents in my late twenties, one morning I came upon my mother sitting in her usual chair, nearest the kitchen, at the end of the dining room table. The cup of hot coffee she poured every morning at six had since cooled, but her hand now repeatedly lifted it, as it would throughout the morning, until there were only grounds and a faint odor. The room was dim and cool from the rhododendrons beyond the bay window, while behind me as I came through the doorway, the kitchen was bright with sun.

As if she'd been thinking of something (which remained un-shared), she emphatically said to me, with conviction and no preface, "I love myself." No more, just another sip. I wondered if my father had gone through and said something that needed this self-affirmation, but I didn't ask.

When at forty-eight I joined *A Course in Miracles*, a spiritual study group, I read that, "God is but love, and therefore so am I."[2] Remembering my mother's unexplained words, I now knew that to love myself was to love God within me.

My father's words came years later. He said, "We never change, we only change our clothes"—nothing further. The sun was lowering on the front side of the Rhode Island home my parents had moved to, where my father now sat in the Swedish-yellow chair by the living room's broad-paned window. Beyond was a curved walk to the driveway and a distant stone wall. My partner Stephen and I, ending our visit, had a two-hour drive ahead, and I was nearly ready to leave. Passing through the hall, I abruptly stopped, hearing my father's words from the living room, directed to me, "We never change, we only change our clothes."

"Of course we change," I shot back, thinking of the years of effort I'd put into seeing counselors, reading self-help books, going to support group meetings, attending *A Course in Miracles* and Hope Community Church. He repeated himself, knowingly smiling. And I knew it really *was* time to go.

I was fifty-four when I began turning in a new direction, finding the truth of my father's words in those of Meher Baba, "Death is like throwing away clothes that have become useless through wear and tear. Just as a traveler may stop at different places, and at each halt may change clothes according to his needs, so the individual goes on changing bodies according to the needs of his sanskaras."[3]

How impeccably God had been leading me on a journey of curving paths.

1953
WIND

A girl not knowing
what to do
that day at the farm,
I just sat
next to the barn
where it turned a corner
to the unused pig yard,
and listened
to flat,
spring-green bamboo
with skin-thin edges
make silk-sounds
on the placid, white clapboards.
When I was fifty,
I read that the wind
was God talking.
I guess God,
not knowing what to do
that day too,
was talking to me.

PJC   1990s

CHAPTER 4

Marriage and Children

1964–1986

Our prayer of thanks

For the laughter of children who tumble barefooted
and bareheaded in the summer grass.[1]

Carl Sandburg

BAR HARBOR

So we broke branches off a bush with blueberries, and holding hands, we carried them trailing through the warm air in our free hands and walked on. Past rough bark of the scrub pines, needles pricking the edges of our sandled feet, down a slope where, laughing, you said, "I'll help you," then fell.

I wondered aloud, "What kind of help is that?"

Up and off, stopping to hear a kinglet or watch a monarch poised on milkweed, we talked rambling thoughts, or just felt the slight pressure of our hands. This was our first summer together.

Through a clearing, onto a stretch of sheltered beach, we kneeled to rest by a pile of clam shells, and breaking several, wrote our names in big, sweeping letters, knowing the low tide would take them before the day ended. Your skin reddened under the sun, as you'd taken off your tee shirt, and across my forehead perspiration wet down long strands of my hair, blowing awry in a salt breeze.

"Promise," you said, and I said, "No," knowing that I had.

But I wasn't going to let you know.

"Race you to the water," I called, dragging my feet free of straps, digging my toes into the ridgy sand. Up to my knees in cold, tangy waves, I lunged out beyond my reach into a shallow dive, calling, "Last one..." my voice trailing off. That was the first time we made love.

PJC   1962

Who was I that autumn of 1964? Newly married to Paul, who I had admired then loved from the first week of our university freshman year, I was about to begin a teaching job not in my field after a summer course of preparation. We were living in Burlington, Vermont, in a too small, second-floor apartment of a brick house with a little grass for a yard. Paul's composure had him well adjusted to a position at the University of Vermont for his second of three college degrees (mathematics, psychology, and management) that by 1968 would culminate in a doctorate from Michigan State University.[1]

Educated to teach high school French, I plumbed my creativity to teach math, science, and Vermont history in a rural grade school—in the mornings to the sixth graders who were slower learners—making cookies and knitting hats to reward them—then teaching the same subjects to the rest of the class in the afternoon. I felt more competent at homemaking, yet opening the refrigerator one day to a bad smell, I needed a neighbor to tell me I'd kept the fresh chicken too long. Homesick by Thanksgiving, I drove us to my parents' for a good turkey dinner, where my already feverish husband spent the day in bed needing not to have come.

During this first teaching job, I developed a desperate need for God's help. In my childhood home there had been no talk of God that I remembered, although I attended Sunday school and church. Now, for a brief period of time, I imagined a small person a quarter of an inch high (God) on my arm, helping me.[2] It would be comical but for the anxiety that drove my misguided effort to soothe my growing sense of failure, making it more worthy of compassion.

By February, a mural of evolution painted by the children in bright poster paint was taped at the top of three sides of the room, and later mounted in the cafeteria, but I was far behind schedule getting through their books. Physically and emotionally drained, when my jaw clamped shut one day and my teeth would not stop grinding, I left school, not to return. On my bed that night, my body shook until the weight of my husband lying on me quieted the spasms. I made an appointment to talk with a psychiatrist, and had I been able to look at an emotional x-ray of myself, I would have been startled to see a three-year-old inside, unable to cope in an adult world. I might have stayed for treatment, but the doctor was so composed, and I felt so out-of-control, I was unable to trust him. Secluded at home, I waited for my symptoms to abate, feeling a failure.

After my abrupt departure from that first teaching job, I had recovered by using the only sentence I remembered from my visit to the psychiatrist. Most people, he'd told me, were doing too much or too little. So I'd found a less demanding job selling women's clothing in a small, family-run store. Five months later, I received a phone call offering me a teaching position for three levels of French at Montpelier High School, and I left, after upsetting the store's owner, who I'd told that I would not be returning to teaching.

We moved to Montpelier over a weekend and into a third-floor apartment under the mansard roof of an older house known as the Gleason House, built in the 1800s. It was on the corner of Spring Street with the Winooski River at the edge of the field-grass lawn and within walking distance of the high school. With twin beds and posts as tall as I was, the mattresses were so high that I had to get on my toes and make a little jump to get on mine. Settled into teaching, I enjoyed my approach for levels one and two of the audio-lingual method of French, but I couldn't easily interpret level three literature. When the principal asked that I teach level four, I quickly refused, which strongly upset him. Every night I fell asleep before 7:30, but restlessly alert at midnight and planning my lessons in the air, I needed a drug store tablet to get back to sleep. Paul commuted forty miles each

way to the University of Vermont and ate dinners from cans he
helped to open. Completing that year taught me that I could not
teach and have a family too. I felt proud of my accomplishments
but left carrying the seed that would reappear in my future of
having chosen the wrong profession.

That summer, before we moved from Vermont to Michigan for
Paul's final degree, we toured Europe, using my teaching income.
While in France, I used my knowledge of the country, but especially of Paris, as I'd put up a large map that my students and I
had studied during the final week of school. Once there, I could
casually say to Paul, "We turn right here for the Gare Saint-Laz-
are," the large railway station in the shopping district that artists
painted and writers wrote about. Among all that I saw during
those six weeks, two memories remain as having unrecognized
meaning for my spiritual journey, a journey as yet unknown to
me. The first was seeing Pope Paul VI in the Vatican, with all its
opulence, and even though Catholicism was not a part of my life,
experiencing the reverence the enormous number of people waiting for him held, their gazes following him as he slowly walked
by. The second was watching the widows of Brittany, recognizing them because they wore only black, with my thought then
of their being alone, but now of the unity of their clothing from
which they might have gathered a feeling of peace.

What I remember of our next home in East Lansing, Michigan, with Paul an Ed.D. candidate at Michigan State University, is mostly without color. I didn't relate well to the flat land,
the monotonously same married student housing, to my master's
level class in French literature, or to substituting. An unplanned
pregnancy that ended in a miscarriage before Christmas was the
beginning of our thinking that we were ready to have children,
but the delay of four years that followed was for the best. The
fond memories that remain are our stay on the first floor of a
small house with a small yard. I can still see Paul across the street,

back bent forward, legs angled and thrusting behind as he pushed the hand mower belonging to our elderly neighbor, helping her to keep her grass trimmed. I would sit on our undistinguished grass happily weeding a long, overgrown bed of purple iris until there were only the tall, narrow, shallow-curved and spear-like leaves and the wings of closed petals raised above, while open and rounding outwardly below—memories that reveal my love for nature and my need for nature's nurturing role.

Throughout Paul's first postgraduate position at George Washington University in Washington D.C., we lived in one of the adjoining John Lenthall houses on 19th Street between F and G two blocks west of the White House. I don't remember being aware of their full historical significance then but I am now. Having the walls painted white for our new Scandinavian furniture was fine, but selecting marine-blue for the kitchen cabinets lacked appropriateness. I was grateful to learn that in 1978 the historical houses were relocated and restored, allaying my regret about that paint.

It was in Washington where I first found opportunities that caused me to begin to bloom, like the cherry trees that bloomed seemingly overnight in mid-March and remained beautiful into April along the avenues. I grew with new freedom, surrounded by acres of refreshing grass on the National Mall. We added a Doberman puppy that I walked around the White House every day, aware of how special that was. For several months I volunteered at the National Collection of Fine Arts as a docent, seated at a desk on the second floor, periodically strolling by the American painters that lined the long room, noting names and styles. I liked 20th century Edward Hopper's realist paintings, and had my favorite. I'd stand for minutes looking; it took me to my grandparents' state of Maine—I'd seen so many views like this one. A white farmhouse, singled out and alone at the top of a hill surrounded by fields, sat close to a narrow road where it began its downward curve.

Then came a turning point. Through a newspaper ad, I met Carol McCabe, a single mother and journalist living in George-town who needed her daughters, two and three, cared for. The first time I entered her small living room, I fell in love with its feeling. A sofa and two comfortable chairs were covered in sunny yellow. As I gazed around, I saw an envelope propped on a narrow shelf, with the return address of Thomas Woolfe, a writer's name that I recognized. Carol was a new kind of woman in my life, and only now have I realized that she was the first writer I knew. She was a one-of-a-kind journalist whose subsequent Rhode Island newspaper stories became my parents' favorites that occasionally found their way into my mailbox. When I found a "special" to *The Washington Post* by her in 2007, I immediately recognized her unique voice and style.[3]

One day, walking down Wisconsin Avenue in Georgetown, I entered The Store Ltd. where bolts of Marimekko fabric were draped over rods on the back wall. Designed in Finland, the patterns were bold, bright, simple, and oversized with the recog-nizable poppy from 1964 still in production. Purchasing several yards and following a necktie pattern, I took some back and the store sold them, with Ethel Kennedy buying several. As our fur-niture had come from Scan, a large store of Scandinavian fur-niture that also carried Marimekko, I approached them as well, and they ordered hundreds. With this larger order, I moved the necktie production to Maine where a family member supervised it. When the neckties arrived, Scan asked to use my name in its *The Washington Post* ad, and I said no—but later wished I'd said yes. (Why I said no so quickly I don't understand... perhaps if I'd felt more self-confident....) But I enjoyed the organizing, and when we moved back east, I found the garment district in lower Manhattan where at a tie shop, ladies with "flying fingers" did the stitching and then I did the shipping. A family member, after receiving one, forever after wore only my Marimekko neckties.

From Washington, we moved to Bloomfield, New Jersey where Paul worked at a small college, and I returned to teaching, developing a new adult school program for English as a Second Language. Although my self-confidence increased, I still had not yet found my niche.

Throughout these four years, Paul and I would have welcomed children. In Washington, then in New York City, infertility studies had been part of our effort. When Paul's friend and faculty member peer and his wife introduced us to their newly adopted five-year-old daughter, seeing their smiles and affected by their joy, within a year we adopted our five-year-old daughter, Beth.

In 1972, the first year Beth expanded our family of two to three, I taught her to ride a bike, bunching the back of her jacket in my hand and running beside her down the long driveway until she could pedal straight and ride with her new neighborhood friends. In 1973, we bought a cottage on Cape Cod, had to move out of our college-rented home, and I became pregnant. Then we bought our own home in Montclair, New Jersey, an old one we could restore, across from Edgemont Park, complete with a pond. Twenty-one months after adopting Beth, Megan was born, and I understood that besides the gift of being our daughter, Beth had been teaching me how to be a mother.

For years, Paul and I and our young daughters crossed Massachusetts' Sagamore Bridge onto Cape Cod to a sand road in Dennisport near South Village Beach and our weathered, gray-shingled cottage, Bay Leaf. There, the double lot had scrub pines, with one supporting a much-used swing.

I think of our daughters' photo—one daughter at six months and the other daughter at seven years—with their dad at the beach—the sun in a milk-blue sky lighting each face. Beth in a navy jersey with her sea-soaked hair in elastics and smiling at the camera sits beside her dad. He is also smiling as he holds Megan against his knee. Wearing a white jersey jumpsuit with a red tie, she stares seriously out to sea, her feet solid on sand. That was the kind of day I knew as happy.

SOUTH VILLAGE BEACH

Waves of a lion's outstretched paws
slap the shore
in a long, low *roar*,
then slinking and *clinking* out over shells
twirl ruffled skirts to a buoy's *bell*.

PJC 1974

CHAPTER 5

First Poetry

1974–1981

I have written in *Writing Alone and with Others*
that there is one acid test for the health of
any group, class, or workshop one might try:
When I leave,
do I feel more like writing,
or less like writing?[1]
Pat Schneider

In Montclair, eight months after Megan was born, I wrote my first poem, inspired by Beth, who was in second grade. Her teacher had a grant for a poet-in-residence who understood how to free children to write poetry and feel good about their poems. Aglow with self-confidence, Beth handed me hers.

Roses are red
Spaghetti is blue
And I love you

I let her know how much love I felt in it.

Her next poem was five lines—a cinquain. I eagerly read it and wrote my own. Beth was my first writing teacher. Seven years later, in a writing workshop, I learned that William Wordsworth, the nineteenth-century poet, had defined poetry as "emotion recollected in a state of tranquility."[2] Writing her first poem, our daughter had suggested a comparison (spaghetti and love) without knowing that she was using a metaphor. Writing the poem taught her that she was a poet, and through her, that *I* was a poet and through my sending my cinquain to my seventeen-year-old brother who wrote *his*, that he was a poet.

Elizabeth McKim and Judith W. Steinbergh write, "Poetry is a special way of perceiving the world. It is a weaving together of feelings and environment. Poets not only see things in great detail, but also see them on other levels.... In order to write poetry, one must be vulnerable, sensitive to sounds and rhythms both in language and in the surrounding environment."[3]

My early poems, "The Gift" and "I Love You," were soon published. Then, upset by the situation of having to see more than one doctor at that time, I wrote a strong poem in which I discovered the words coming in a rush, without thought. I can still feel the inescapable emotion in my inflection and in the rhythm of the words coming together when I remember it. That poem gave birth to a desk for writing in a small, unused room on our second floor. Meeting with poet Toi Derricotte, who lived nearby, she told me that I needed to go beyond writing in my kitchen and into New York City. When writing this book, I came to understand that she too had been at a turning point in her life, as I discovered that she was then on the brink of becoming a nationally known and respected poet with the publication of her first major book of poetry just two years later in 1978, *The Empress of the Death House*.[4]

By 1976, I was driving at night through the Lincoln Tunnel to New York University's Washington Square Writing Center for a class in advanced poetry writing. Forty years later, I felt affirmed that I had kept writing, putting those early emotions on paper, when I read these words by Pat Schneider in her book *How the Light Gets In: Writing as a Spiritual Practice*, "The power of writing to heal is being widely studied and affirmed. What those of us who have written at our kitchen tables and in our shops and offices have always known by heart is now being acknowledged by study and evidence in centers of science and medicine."[5]

In 1977, when our daughters were eleven and three, Paul's next position required a move to Western Massachusetts. In the following chapter, there is more about our new family life, but I will mention here that on our first day on Birnie Road in Longmeadow, neighbor Candy came to say hello and to let us know that her daughters were three and four, discovering with pleasure that we had a three-year-old daughter. And from across the road, Helen and Harlan, retired Longmeadow residents for many years, eagerly welcomed us, obviously happy at the new circumstance of additional children on our road. From then on Helen would invite us into her kitchen, and in the warmth of her personality, she soon seemed like a long-time friend. Harlan, in a hearty voice, regularly called across the road for us to come visit him at the round, white table where he routinely sat passing the day under a tilted umbrella.

I continued writing on a typewriter that Megan wrote to me about this past year, surprising me by her memory of how she had been fascinated by the white paper I used to make corrections. After three years, with great excitement I received a letter saying that I had been accepted at Bread Loaf Writers' Conference in Middlebury, Vermont. Held in summer, I was not only thrilled to be in classes led by major American poets, but at the college I was surrounded by green everywhere, and it was picturesquely beautiful. The only poem I can now remember submitting was a villanelle (a poem of nineteen lines with only two rhymes throughout and some lines repeated), so perhaps it was my effort at this more difficult form plus having two published poems and my exposure to the Washington Square Writing Center that gave me this opportunity.

During those two weeks I had two experiences that made opposite but lasting impressions. As one class began, nationally known poet Linda Pastan, whose poetry I liked, read aloud my villanelle, which began, "Earth and sun and water make beans grow ...," then in a voice projected over our heads announced that *this* was an example of what a villanelle was not! Singled out in an uncaring way for failure, I felt isolated in a room of writers who, I imagined, were better than I was, and where everyone now knew that I didn't meet the standards for being there.

Twenty years later I was able to put my experience into perspective through reading *Redirecting Children's Behavior*. The characteristics of a first child are that she "needs to feel right, perfect, [and] superior,"[6] so she needs to be taught that mistakes are for learning and that being gentle with herself is how to accept failure—the way I was treating myself by then.

Fate had its kindness too. On one afternoon, I was sauntering along a path bordered with touch-me-not bushes with Howard

Nemerov, who served as the Poet Laureate Consultant to the Library of Congress in the 1960s and would again in the 1980s. Older, kindly spoken, quiet in speech, and willing to share his time with a relatively new writer, we had parted with his saying, "Courage," and inviting me to send him poems, if I wanted. Graciously returning comments on several that I did send to him, by his small attentions, he encouraged me to continue writing, and when later the *New York Quarterly* accepted my poem "Ripening," in gratitude, I wished that he could have known.

Next I discovered Pat Schneider's writing workshops in Amherst, Massachusetts, which I describe in greater detail in "Finding My Niche." In a phone call, remembered to this day, I ended it by telling her that I'd like to come to one of her workshops, never guessing at the time how much they would change my life. My route to her home, at dusk, was poetry itself—the Connecticut River appearing and disappearing, seasonal fields, a small town with a library building. Then I was parking on McClellan Street and walking to the open inside door of the front porch of an older home. A passing glance through a doorway showed me a piano, and at the end of the narrow hallway, I could see people standing and sitting, getting ready to write in a room of books and soft lamplight. Finding Pat to introduce myself, she immediately made me feel as comfortable as if I'd been coming for years. Seeing that the rocking chair wasn't taken, I sat and put my writing pad on my lap, waiting.

That night I knew Pat only as the founder of Amherst Writers & Artists, but later, in one of her books, I read how she must have seen us seated around her: "You have a voice, just as surely as you have a face, and it is already full of character, passionate and nuanced and beautiful."[7] Becoming a regular in her workshops, I learned of more than her literary accomplishments. I experienced her writing with us and sharing her writing, her telling us of her rejections as well as her publications. Without ever referring to "unconditional love," she maintained a safe space where responses to new writing were only our answers to, "Folks, what do you like? What do you remember?" I was still writing with her ten years later when I heard the words unconditional love spoken in a spiritual study group, *A Course in Miracles*, and recognized that Pat's method had already established the beginnings of that love within me.

THE GIFT

From your favorite daughter
here's a picture made for you
of crayon love and paper
and sticky, white glue.

PJC 1974

I LOVE YOU

Peaches and cream, strawberry ice cream,
damp, warm-blushed cheek seeking mine—
so cool.

Mother love meets daughter love
in the shelter-seeking world
of sleeplessness.

Hesitant steps, outstretched arms
to soft snuggling, leaving me whispering,
"Strawberry ice cream, I love you."

PJC 1974

MERRY-GO-ROUND *Song*

Up and down on the merry-go-round,
   Calliope whistling a merry-go-sound,
   Ride on a dapple gray, gallop through air,

Reins lightly slapping a merry-go-mare.
   High-arched tails and glossy manes flare,
   Bold horses grin at the merry-go-scare.
   A circle of children who've come to the fair,

Wait for a ride on the merry-go-there.

PJC 1975

CHANGING

CHAPTER 6

Beginnings and Endings

1977–1989

Often it takes a real crisis to bring out
A sure knowledge of the real inner self
And it is always a creative knowledge.[1]

Meher Baba

In our new home, we each had different themes in our lives. Paul had begun in administration at a new college, Beth would begin at a middle school, while Megan and I were getting to know a neighbor and her daughter who was Megan's age, and discovering our new town. Paul's accomplishments at the college, our daughters, our home and yard became the core of my life. My role as a grateful mother carried me through these years, but my role as Paul's wife would produce varying emotions.

We had found a "carpenter's special" two houses from Longmeadow Street where Beth could get her bus to Glenbrook Middle School, and Megan, in two years, could walk across the town green on her own under my supervision to kindergarten at Center School. In the winters when she went to Bay Path Pre-School a mile away, I pulled her on her sled over the snow-packed sidewalks. Each summer I grew a small garden where the girls watched green tomatoes ripen (and smelled them). At seven, Megan made a scarecrow dressed in a sundress, long-sleeved jersey, and doll's bonnet, which tilted behind the knee-high sunflowers as she raked the grass around the edges.

I encouraged our daughters to make their own decisions. Throughout my own fifth grade year, each day I'd find my school dress hanging on my closet doorknob, then stand as my mother first took out the metal rollers that curled my hair under and then combed it. When Beth told me she'd take off a top I'd made when she got to school, I thought of her as independent. When Megan chose her outfits for school and costumes for play, I saw her originality—one time, pasting short, paper feathers over her body and wearing a beak, she crouched on the ground for my camera to record her as a bird.

During that first year, I found focus in our family life, and with Paul, spent months tearing out the kitchen (and as a result, washed dishes in the bathtub upstairs), then implementing our design part by part. It was the kind of work that we did well together. There would be an L-shaped counter under double windows that looked to the west at our neighbor's large, split-leaf maple, and a glass sliding door bringing in the small backyard. We'd keep the garage for lack of money and for its added charm of being old. Beyond it we could see woods, extending from the Thomas's farther down Birnie Road, and to the bottom of Harry's yard, where a long-lived, Baldwin apple tree on the other side of the occasionally trimmed, sparse hedge gave us appealing privacy.

After our first year in this house, I had become unsettled. My behavior changed in unimagined ways not consistent with my family values that I would not understand for many years. What I had learned in Montpelier (I could have a family or teach) was a seed thought that now began to grow. Family had been my choice. But my thoughts were increasingly focused on the unreality of my chosen profession, which was to teach French at the middle school level. Requirements had changed, including an ability to also teach English or Spanish, for which I was not certified.

I had no idea of what I could do if I needed to work—even though there was no indication I might have to. But my anxiety kept increasing. My husband and daughters were only aware that I was at my typewriter a lot, but I knew that I missed being with other writers weekly. As a result, I held on tighter to my home and yard and my role as a mother as my sources of safety and as a way for me hold my focus while Paul concentrated on his career.

So, when an unexpected letter arrived, surprising me as I found its content inappropriate, I didn't realize that my reaction indicated a blind spot of mine. The letter was likely a delayed response to one of mine to a former poetry teacher. The inspiration for the letter had been a scene that I'd witnessed at our bird feeder. Horrified, I'd stood mesmerized and immobile as I watched a cat shoot out from under a bush, clawing a squirrel and spattering blood over the snow in their squalling fight. This brutal reality of nature struck my sensibility with a teaching to which I responded from a depth never before felt. My suppressed experiences of fear about death emerged, and I wrote a long poem on the attack and my emotions, which I sent to this poetry teacher who would understand that I was processing my human shattering.

I hadn't expected a reply. I understand now that the man, a teacher of writers who was older and wiser and more experienced, recognized that I was seeking my identity through writing. My emotional immaturity and vulnerability were apparent to him.

Suffering from fear that went far beyond the lines of the poem, I wasn't helped by my mother, who asked what could be wrong, as I had a home and a family, or my father who in frustration asked if I needed a kick in the ass, or needed more reminders of my accomplishments. I didn't know what was wrong with me. My anger erupted against my parents and my husband as I tried to rid myself of my suffering by blaming them. It felt both appropriate and justified, but below the surface it would grow into a bog of guilt. The day I drove after Paul eighty miles an hour down the highway because I was angry and he refused further talk was a splitting between the adult I could be in most situations and the emotional child momentarily in control. Finally, in one conversation, Paul used a metaphor that I could understand. He told me that I had "the appetizer, the salad, and the dessert, but not the main meal." He understood a lot about me, but was personally unable to help me.

In the months that followed, my former teacher and I exchanged occasional letters, and I began to feel understood by him. As a result, I naïvely believed that I could add a life with him to my life with Paul. So without separating from Paul, I began making several visits to my former teacher in Greenwich Village, where the lifestyle, the classes he took me to, the absence of time, day or night, our walks through the streets—all were new and exciting adventures, and I, oblivious, had the thought that I had two husbands.

I was simply unable to separate reality from fantasy. In my un-knowing, I chose to be open about my New York life with Paul, causing him great pain. But he could see that I was writing more and more, causing him to hang on. It was his maturity and constancy that kept our family together.

WHEN WE MET

I should have put a seed in your hand,
made your fingers rain
on a small, dun-colored reminder.
A seed extends a root no thicker than string.
Heart bare, a seed sends up a living rocket,
et voilà two false leaves,
et voilà, two real leaves.

There are trees older than the birth of Jesus,
trees that will live until space is colonized.
A beech tree was my mother.
I knew a man raised by a birch.
The locust has thorns and a bridal veil of blossoms.
Put a swing rope on the maple. It's your red umbrella.
Bury the dog under the white pine so fallen needles
remind you that his fur was coppery.

A foot tall, our love cast a small shadow.
Your hand danced toward the smooth bark.
Under a canopy of lime leaves we were lovers.
Seven years have produced a trunk to lean on.
I offer my simple friendship. Yet you question me.
I should have put a...now
open your hand.

PJC 1985

My fantasy ended a year and a half later in a cold, pouring rain on a city street, where I stood with little protection under the open-grill of black metal steps above my head. In a flash of clarity, I said, "I am missing my dear Cordelia," my feelings drawn from the emotions of King Lear in Shakespeare's play. In sudden awareness, my vision had cleared, and I realized what I had risked. Overwhelmed by longing, I returned home that final weekend, ashamed, as a period of confusion ended and I sought to mend the damage to my family and repair myself.

"You need help," Paul said, as for the second time in my marriage to him I was unable to cope. This time I found a clinic and went weekly to talk to a psychiatrist. He would lean back in his chair, non-responsive, balancing his new, white sneakers on the desk while I talked, and my increasing dislike of him became a positive strength, prompting me to find a woman psychologist with whom I would work, as needed, over eight years.

We did reach a time when we needed money, and letting go of my pride, I took a job in Beth's middle school cafeteria. In retrospect, it was the best situation that could have taken place. Making bologna sandwiches and putting dishes through the dishwasher, I watched the lunch ladies, learning how professional they were. Still taking an antidepressant that I would soon stop, I sat alone on our lunch hour until I nearly lost my job, but spoken to, improved my behavior and finished the year pleased, looking for other ways to earn money. I had, through commitment to my family, breached the gap of not knowing what I could do for work—an important step in building the self-esteem for work that I lacked.

When I approached the manager of the Friendly's Ice Cream Shop that was within walking distance from our home, he hired me for part-time hours. While I gave him my real name, I wrote Colette (in honor of the French writer) on my badge. I discovered I liked serving hamburgers and scooping ice cream, especially when Paul brought five-year-old Megan for a cone. Growing in self-confidence, I was breaking away from what I had imagined my life would be.

During this time, Paul experienced a transition in his career, and unable to find a position in our area and liking our new town and home and the educational opportunities for our daughters, he put aside the skills for administrative positions at institutions of higher learning. For the next several years, he began to build college and university bookstores designed by a friend he'd met at the University of Vermont. His absence from our home would ultimately change the stability of our marriage; however the carpentry opportunity that kept him on the road five and a half days a week would later prove to be of future significance in his life in more than one way. His presence at the colleges and universities would put him in contact with administrators in a new kind of relationship. The final outcome was that he discovered he had abilities in drafting and designing that he added to his years of experience in administration.

As he increasingly represented his designer friend's business interests on the job sites better than his friend could (who though highly talented could be blunt), Paul became known not only for his organization of the renovation of the bookstores, but also for his friendly, story-telling personality, backed up by his doctorate in education. When he was offered what for us was a healthy sum of money to begin his own business, we said, "Yes!" even though that amount was to be repaid at three times the investment. Beth was to start her university freshman year, but I said she could work for a year, if necessary (it proved not to be), as Paul, in his mid-forties, deserved to be supported first. We used our family home and summer cottage as collateral with no thought of failure knowing that Paul could do this.

Through my therapy with the psychologist, our marriage entered a period of healing. As my salary was supporting us, Beth qualified for scholarships and loans, and in 1984 entered the University of Rhode Island. Paul gave me a silver and turquoise cloisonné ring that I loved as beautiful and unique and wore on my wedding finger. I felt deeply grateful as he succeeded at each design job he received. He had found his niche after having to leave university positions where his insightful views had made him more maverick than game player, while I had viewed him as brilliant, talented, and hardworking. And it was during this period in the mid-eighties that my poems "Flowers," "Harry's Apples," and "Monet's Water Lilies" were written in a return to the good relations that Paul and I had experienced during the first year in our home.

FLOWERS

In the breeze, marigold,
cosmos, dianthus buds
play on the garden's green sea,
tight mouths nursed by the sun.
Stems that make a ruffled fence
resist my scissors
but can't keep in the fragrance.
Tiger-striped, a bee
buzzes in a poppy's bowl
of orange light.

HARRY'S APPLES

I hear the thud from my backyard and smile—Harry's apples. A hedge divides his yard from ours. The clouds are distant, and grass rises wet and stringy over my sneakers as I walk determinedly toward the corner where our lots meet. Here my hips part the hedge as I enter the world of apples. It's an old tree—Harry's—at the foot of his large, sloping yard. The Y opens with stout arms at angles anyone could climb onto. Yet, this is a standing-under-tree, for now it isn't clouds but leaves above me.

These Baldwins are hard to see greening in the shadows, but, ah, beneath my feet it's different. Here a sea of apples anchors the ground, a motley crowd abused by earth banging, scavenging raccoons and woodchucks, slugs, ants, and me. Oh, some are all red with a galaxy of white dots scattered over them. Maybe there's a black welt, or scabby hole, or torn stem. Others have a top eruption of pale, watery-green that stains the sides with rivulets searching down the curve of the small, sweet-scented fruit. This one I pick up has slugs at work. I brush them off with my fingertip. Another has a spongy hole, tea-brown, and warns of some creature having eaten there that maybe hasn't left.

Harry's away and since his wife died last year, no one's come to pick up apples for pies and sauce. I fill my large yellow bowl—a pyramid of apples—apples that tumble off as I walk. I struggle, arms and hands filled with Harry's apples, through the back door of my kitchen.

Is it ritual or religion that has me bringing home apples every year to cook and season and store in spiced and lumpy servings so the winter applesauce will be fresh in the dish? The cooking steam carries apples to the attic. In the kitchen, the family stops to smell the cooking apples. The hot mush turns white fruit and red skins to pink. The chunks grow smaller. The whole, when done, must be forced by hand crank through the fine holes of the food mill to make it more than liquid, less than chewy flesh.

Thud! Another apple's hit the ground, the fall of fruit—ripe or unripe, weakened and dropping early. Again, I hear a thud. In my imagination, Harry appears. "These apples—you can have them." His figure disappears. I take the apples as communion. I see Harry's hands caring for his yard. Shadows of red and black and green enter me. The sky is too far away to speak. The thud of apples falling—someone is calling me.

PJC   1984

MONET'S WATER LILIES

After viewing Brancusi and Picasso,
I climb to MoMA's third floor. Manhattan
is at my back. I am a suburban fish
come to visit great art. Sounds of car
horns, accelerating buses, and strange
voices are the cost of the trip.

I put notebook aside and step into an aqua
boat in the dappled light of Giverny.
I listen to water plap, hear bee hum,
watch insects skitter over the palish pond.
I lean toward the liquid, lucent pastels
and become one with the approachable
calm of water lilies.

PJC   1985

When a significant increase in our income came, Paul took his newfound money and bought a blue Jetta, and I used my newly freed-up income to buy a sand-colored Saab. Eventually, he achieved national and international recognition. Excited for him and proud of his designing, I created a business Christmas card for him in ink pointillism that showed his hand holding a drawing tool, poised over his drawing board.

It was during my time at Friendly's Ice Cream Shop that I had begun dance classes in tap and jazz at a nearby studio. There, I met Patty who told me about an open position for a paste-up artist at the large newspaper advertising company where she worked in administration. Considering my artistic ability, my interest in graphic arts, and the company's location just over the border in Connecticut, I had applied. I imagine now that for my interview I had taken my latest ink drawing for a fund-raiser with ice cream servings at Megan's elementary school. The "Back to Sundae School" publicity sketch had jungle animals as the "students and parents" attending—an idea that had been pure fun to create.

The fun translated into a job for me. I had been accepted for a thirty-hour workweek but was required to work on a Saturday or on one night. As soon as my brother heard that I had chosen a night shift, he immediately dissuaded me. His effort would further prove right when Paul and I separated, as Megan would have been left alone at night—an unthinkable condition. So I had worked my six-hour shift on Saturdays.

As time went on, the consequence we hadn't anticipated was that with Paul in his new office and on the road again and me in my fourth year at the graphic arts job, which included Saturdays, we only had Sundays as our partial day together. Lacking in communication, a chasm developed, affecting our parenting, which I had hoped we could do together but increasingly were doing separately. I lacked the emotional maturity to bridge the gap with

Paul (also increasingly with Beth), and Paul, understandably, withdrew more into his work.

TO AN ANGRY DAUGHTER

Independent and able to see me
as I could not see myself

Forgive me

   ...for misunderstanding the meaning of your words, which
   was not on the surface, like the red sauce that clung dry to
   the dirty fork in your hand, but in the metal of the fork, the
   sinew handle, the spine of prongs.

   Your bones bent in anger. Breaking stone, words fell from
   your mouth—rasping, gravelly, sharp-edged.

Forgive me

Forgive me

   ...the wind of words that bore witches out of my mouth, out
   of my stomach like a washing machine, out of my intestines
   constipated with desire to control you.

Forgive me

Forgive me

   ...for standing close and telling you not to leave. What I
   meant was, never leave, stay weak as egg white, simple as
   jelly, young as a pullet, ineffectual as dough. I got out the
   umbilical cord and in seconds tried to tie us together again.

Forgive me

Forgive me

   ...as I paint explanations of how my way to see a thing is
      broad, experienced, mature—yet falsely so and fearful of
      your self-assured, your self-reliant...your
      young woman's way.

Forgive me

Forgive me

   ...as I love the metal of your eyes. As you knew an insult
      when you heard one.
      As I love the light in your eyes—rich, crystal shadows
      of brown.

Forgive me

                          PJC   1985

A disturbing aspect of our new affluence was a change in my personality. Accustomed to living materially simply for years, I developed inflated ideas. When I was invited in 1988 to read a poem at a conference in Paris, I considered going. That was the year Pan Am Flight 103, traveling from Frankfort to Detroit, crashed in Lockerbie, Scotland, destroyed by a terrorist bomb. My family asked me not to go but still I debated, and while I finally decided not to go, there was a lag in my response that I later saw as insensitivity to their concern. I read of an art exhibit of French impressionism being shown in California and thought of going. But it was my talk of buying a new house that was the most extreme, even identifying an area that had available lots in a location that could not compare to our unmatched one off the Longmeadow green. I was out of control. I did return to the University of Maine to attend a National Poetry Foundation conference, with my intention being to hear contemporary poetry and participate in the readings. I remember Bob Creeley, a well-known poet and author usually associated with the Black Mountain poets, being there because in the auditorium after I had read "Harry's Apples," he found me to say that he liked it. But I returned home aware that I had met another conference attendee who had caused a response in me that could, and did, affect my marriage, as if reaching the pinnacle of losing who I had been, I was struggling toward something undefined that was pulling me on.

It would be many years before I understood that my accomplishments hid the insecurities I continued to carry, all of which I had brought to my marriage. Had I known that my need to find parts of myself by a long and arduous journey, unknown except by living it, would bruise my family and ultimately me, I might not have begun it; but had I not, I might have permanently remained an emotionally immature child in an adult body.

The psychologist I had worked with during this time period,

near the end of my treatment, wrote a brief description, which I asked for, that used the term "lack of individuation." She told me that because my emotions were so strong she had intentionally provided a space where I could release them, but that just knowing this didn't mean that I would change. That turned out to be true. As Paul and I faced the ending of our marriage, he told me that I had always wanted him to be different. For the first time I understood what he was saying and that something was very wrong in that.

Two and a half years after I ended my marriage, I was the one left as the other closed the door. I became short-tempered with the Indian girl I tutored at the high school, and she pointed that out. One morning I got out of bed and then back in bed and then out again, unable to decide, as my daughters, who were ready for school and work, watched with concern from my door. "Call her," I said, when my older daughter asked about my psychologist. After the call, my daughter returned to my room to tell me that if I could make the decision to go into the hospital, it would be better for me.

BEYOND REACH

My daughters stand at my door.
I can't get out of bed.
Three times I've tried,
but each time I turn
and put my head
back on the pillow.
I've never closed my mind
to morning—
forgotten how
yellow forsythia
waits out winter,
cupped in leaves,
or thin, sweet cocoa
helps me struggle out of ache.
"What do you want us to do?"
Can't they read my eyes?
There's no meaning—
like fingers new to Braille.
"I'll call Miriam,"
my older daughter says
and disappears to dial the therapist.
There's nothing to hear
but the phone
ringing beyond my reach.

PJC   1989

The benefit was not visible as we rang the bell and entered the lock-up unit of the psychiatric wing of a hospital in Springfield, this response to my third time of being unable to function. Moved after a week into the residential wing, one day while showering, I saw sudden, blinding flashes of light, something that had happened to me once before when I was in junior high, but this time they brought me to my knees. Crawling to my bed I rang the bell. The doctor said it was a drug reaction. I knew that he was wrong even though at that point, I did not know what *had* actually happened.

It was traumatizing to be locked up. So, with a first small appearance of health, I had negotiated an opportunity to walk the parking lot for short periods, from where I could see the highway. In bleak contrast, I would repeat to myself, "I used to drive to Amherst" and "I've been to Europe." I left the hospital facing the fact that I had a relationship addiction that was codependency, and only years later would I recognize that the flashes had had a spiritual meaning.

And so my recovering began.

CHAPTER 7

Violin, Ballet, Art

1989–1991

Where most might have remarried and worked a
regular job, you've let your unique path unfold.

Megan Sciera

Home.

Standing in my driveway, looking at the lawn that would soon spurt fat, yellow dandelions, and gazing up at the barely-open, light green leaves of the sugar maples, I felt bone-deep relief to be free. Now safe and breathing in fresh air, with my feet firmly on familiar gravel, I said to the trees and to the sky—"There must be a better way." I didn't know that similar words—"There must be another way!"[1] —had already been spoken in 1965 by William Thetford, Director of Clinical Psychology at Columbia-Presbyterian Hospital, to his assistant, research psychologist Helen Schucman, about their being "hyper critical and hyper competitive"[2] with one another. Schucman agreed. Soon afterward, Shucman began hearing an "inner voice of a dream character"[3] she described as Jesus. Encouraged by Thetford, she took notes, and the transcription by both of them became known as *A Course in Miracles.*

During this time, one day I said aloud, "I'm rude," and that caught my attention. Suddenly, by my straightforward confession, I figured out that I acted rudely but rationalized my behavior. My friends disagreed, but I knew I had made a breakthrough; I was no longer hiding. I didn't feel punished, merely informed with new awareness of what I could work on. Eventually I recognized that the learning I needed would come in moments like this.

Creating a safer space for myself began in support groups that I attended from late spring 1989 to the fall of 1990 when I joined *A Course in Miracles.* Paul's few words of my wanting him to be different echoed, as I understood that I was the one who had to change. Secure with Paul's generous child support and staying in the home where our daughters had grown up, I began studying spiritual ways of living. Beth had graduated from the university and lived at home, working locally, while Megan's needs and activities gave me purpose and especially pleasure from her violin, ballet, and art studies.

Thirty years later, I am still on that journey, although with a fuller understanding of how to relate to life situations as who I am. A book by my first editor, Anna Kirwan, rested on my desk for a while because of its title, *The Jewel of Life.*[1] While it refers to a gem in the story of Duffy and Master Crowe, I looked at it as a reminder that life *is* a jewel given.

THE WAY THE DAY BEGINS

in that moment between worlds
when dark lifts like the spirit
from its grave

and pewter banks the winter trees–
scabbed, deformed, their green
taffeta stored;

when breathing is quiet
as distant galaxies and no man's
hand heats my sagging thigh;

faith seeded months ago
blooms in the thin, cold air;
my eyes are open flowers

determined to see the day
new, on the small, square face
of the clock.

PJC   1991

CHAPTER 8

Finding My Niche

1991–1995

According to Jung, the individual's desire
to know the self and reach into the depths
of consciousness is the basis for all story-
telling as we instinctively try to understand
this deeper nature through metaphor.[1]

Lisa Schade Eckert

My first phone call to Pat Schneider, mentioned in "First Poetry," had been tentative. I had felt a desire to return to a weekly writing group, as when I had participated in the Washington Square Writing Center with its positive effects on my writing, but did not wish to repeat the later situation of embarrassment at Bread Loaf Writers' conference that had shown me a kind of teacher I definitely did not want to write with. In my conversation with Pat, I found her understanding of my questioning. Hearing of how she conducted her workshops allayed my concerns and when she said, "Just give yourself the gift of five minutes of writing a day," I heard kindness behind her words, and so in trust I joined her writing community.

The influence of her personally created approach to prompt writing changed my writing practice. Along with writing on my own, I was also now doing writing exercises during group time that had me immediately putting my pen to paper. For the first time, I heard other committed writers' responses to what I read as they pointed out strong elements of my writing that I didn't see. Pat responded also, but only if she had a comment different from what was offered or wanted to emphasize one. By this process of affirming only, a core concept of her writing workshops, each week my growth in awareness of my abilities and my ongoing exposure to the craft of writing was slowly, and gently, increasing. Listening to the writing of others affected my writing in the ways of discovering and developing my own voice. Aligned with my changing writing was a new exploration into the depths of a place within me where there were aspects of needed growth that had not developed nor could have until I found my own identity. By gradually discovering that identity through this new writing, facing it directly or by metaphor, that growth began. What had been tied down in me was being unloosed.

Yet even in the middle of those ten years of safe space, I had
needed to take a two-year leave, blocked to writing by the tran-
sitions I was undergoing. Intuitively, I bought a hardbound art
book and began drawing. Amidst all that drawing, gradually a
few words had appeared (three) until by the end of the book, writing and drawing covered each page. Reading of an Intensive Journal Workshop" in upstate New York, I decided to attend, having
no idea how important it would be as a new turning point. Dr.
Ira Progoff, a practicing depth psychologist, had discovered in his
psychotherapy sessions that his clients who wrote in some form
of a journal were able to work through issues more rapidly, and
from this observation he had created the Progoff *Intensive Journal* Program for Self-Development[2] that emphasizes spiritual as
well as personal growth.

At the workshop I bonded with my roommate in a mystical
way. While walking we would find money, which we decided was
worthy of our attention as it was never only a lucky penny but
quarters. Years later we would meet again at her New Jersey home
returning to our earlier friendship.

One day, as I sat in a session in a large room with over a hundred people, I had a highly unusual experience that I couldn't explain. I had finished writing before most of the other writers and
absent-mindedly stared out a wall of large windows that covered
the length of the room. Before me was a wide view of a restful
scene of grass and a walk mid-point between the building and
where the grass grew far back. My attention was drawn to a single
figure at the far left walking toward the building. I could tell it
was a tall man and could see him more clearly as he approached.
Continuing to watch, I suddenly lost all sense of understanding.
The man was my father! Not a resemblance of my father but my

father. I stared, uncomprehending, until he had passed. This experience would reoccur in the future, and at some point I asked myself why I never approached these exact resemblances, but I never did. After the session, I called my father in Rhode Island, and he reassured me that he was in Rhode Island and not in upstate New York, and then asked why I was calling. Not until 2018 did I learn from one of my spiritual teachers that *my* "spirit" might begin to appear elsewhere, and *I* would be seen as being there. In truth, this had already happened. A previous neighbor had emailed that he had seen me at his church in Florida when I was in India. Looking back, I now understood that it was my father's spirit I had seen. My father was the first, but there would be others I saw in their exact appearance.

The *Intensive Journal Workshop* was my first meeting with spirituality, although at the time I wasn't conscious of this. The only writing I remember is a piece I wrote called "Twilight Imagery" that suggests I had an unknown ability, thus making a first connection with this part of my life. Returning from the workshop, I wrote two thousand words, as what had been blocking my writing had broken free. Calling Pat, I returned to my regular Thursday night workshop, which was the longest running group with mostly the same, familiar members. Pat writes, "It takes both honesty and courage to try to wrestle the truth of experience onto a page. But in writing it, we come to understand what we didn't understand before."³ And I had done that.

During the winter of 1991, as I was leaving the writing workshop one night, Pat handed me a note. I didn't read it until two a.m. in my bedroom with only the bushes beyond my window sharing my moments. What I read altered my calm. I went from amazement to joy—a passage in seconds to my future. Pat had written that she thought I would be good at leading a writing group and suggested a writer's "support group" as I didn't have a master's degree as other leaders did.

My home was a three-quarter colonial with a small yard on a quiet street, an inviting place to come to write. Out front was a large, yellow-leafed sugar maple with a slender red-leafed one by the side porch, and both were near the thinned-out bushes between my yard and the neighbor's expansive lawn. The street was often empty and cars could park in my home's worn-out grass and gravel driveway that led to an old garage.

Thinking of where we would meet, I looked at the living room, with its curved sofa for four, two black leather chairs, lightweight and easy to move, and a rocker, knowing that straight back chairs could be brought in if needed. Writers who liked to work alone could move to an oblong teak table in the dining room or to the kitchen where a red wooden table and benches faced a sliding glass door. From there the view was of woods, an apple tree, coppery needles under pines, and a forsythia bush. A small room beyond the living room's French doors had a secretary desk with the hinged desktop left open and a wall of windows bringing in the outdoors.

Stephen, my second husband but still only a close friend at this point in time, offered to design my logo, letterhead, brochure, and flyers. He organized my ideas with my key words, "writing for self-exploration, health, and artistic expression," my biography, and my publications, setting them in Garamond, a font that he felt suited me perfectly, to which I agreed as soon as I saw it.

I chose a first night date for early summer (this was 1991) and invited my friends to come to help me practice, assuring them that they would be able to write with my exercises. I began collecting objects, used photography and art books that I cut up, and museum postcards, and then wrote on hundreds of three-by-five cards, each with one quotation including the author's name. And at the end of the first night, I faced a roomful of "writers" who'd enjoyed the experience and been surprised by how easy it was to write, and more, had been willing to read their writing. It was after that night that I knew—writing was my mission.

In the beginning, I had two morning groups, nearly filling the quota. But at night only one writer came. Maureen was a journalist for a Springfield newspaper and for six months the two of us wrote, enjoying the closeness of extended writing and our time out for chatting and refreshment. In this intimacy, our writing grew in a different way that redefined itself as the group grew to ten. Hearing about my groups from others, by the end of the first year Pat was recommending my group to people.

At my parents' home for a visit that first year, I had sat thumbing through a stack of magazines, looking at poems and pictures for exercises for my new writing groups. At some point, I found myself staring at the face of a white horse on a magazine cover and, unable to stop myself, tore off the cover, put it in a frame, and placed it on the second shelf above the hinged desktop of my secretary desk where I wrote. Every time I walked by, I looked or paused. I had memories about horses from a young age through high school, yet none explained my strong attraction to the white horse, which would not be revealed for twelve years.

From where I sat in front of the fireplace glass doors, able to watch the front door for latecomers, at 7:30 I brought the group's attention to the exercise. Above me on the wall was a large, single purple flower head rendered in the style of artist Georgia O'Keefe, painted by Megan. In a corner, floor-to-ceiling bookcases held all of my workshop supplies from reference books to literary journals and writing exercise materials.

One week I carried my grandmother Hilda's wooden ironing board into the living room, set it up without a word, returned with a somewhat used man's white shirt, then an iron I'd been heating out of sight, quickly touched my fingertip from tongue to iron, causing a long "hiss," and placing the iron back on the board, sat down and picked up my pen. The first writer to read said, "I have never liked ironing!" The opportunity to write from an exercise, or not, is part of the method, accompanied by an added remark to write your shopping list if nothing comes. I don't ever remember anyone not writing.

In a career counseling session during my second year of writing workshops, my counselor had listened to the tonal quality of my voice to determine what my real interests were. When I told her that I wanted to offer spiritual journaling in my writing community, she asked me to repeat what I had said. I did with no idea of what I meant. But she had identified that this was where my energy lay, and by asking me to repeat, she was having me affirm the importance of my words. I found *Life's Companion: Journal Writing as a Spiritual Quest*[4] by Christina Baldwin with her teaching of being a "walker" and a "watcher" of oneself. Guided by her book, we wrote, exploring ourselves. Often that was enough in itself as at times, my responses to members' writing were simply of my feeling moved.

While Megan was in fourth grade, I had invited her to come with me one night to Pat's workshop. Surprised by her depth of observation in writing, I followed this by inviting young people's writing workshop leader Ani Tuzman[5] to come to our home and give weekly workshops for Megan and her friends. From the ability of these young writers came a cable TV series, *Public Access Poetry*, with the children and invited poet Margaret Robison.[6] Her idea of having seniors write together with the young writers developed into Part One of four interviews I did of Margaret telling stories about her life in Georgia and reading poems from her book, *The Naked Bear*. In Part Two Margaret led four on-camera writing workshops, with the seniors (who had not been in writing workshops before) seated on chairs, and the young writers gathered around her on the floor. In her Georgia drawl, Margaret spoke slowly and quietly, leading her listeners on a journey of words so successfully that when she was finished, all of them picked up their pens and pencils and with the cameras shutting down began to write. When it was time to read, the cameras were turned back on; as each writer finished reading, Margaret smiled, gently asking questions or giving comments, showing all of them her appreciation for their writing.

Captivated now by children's willingness, enthusiasm even, to be open and creative in writing, in the third year of my writing community, I offered a young writers' workshop for children ages six to seven. Given an opportunity to write from exercises they hadn't experienced before, the young writers, not yet able to spell all the words that they knew, wrote phonetically, creating poems and complete stories. Each week they improved as they discovered their previously unknown abilities in a guided freedom of exploration. I was astounded! I typed their writing with correct spelling, also keeping the original versions for each one. I wrote too and listened to six and seven year olds give thoughtful and accurate comments about my writing. The Friday afternoon group was so successful that at six o'clock when it was time to stop, the children didn't want to leave even though their parents were waiting outside. Eventually the young writers' complaint to their teachers that they no longer liked writing at school (most went to a private academy) prompted my being invited by the academy to give their teachers a workshop in a new approach to evoke truly creative children's writing that participants responded to with great interest.

In my fourth year, due to the writing advancement of many of the Longmeadow Writers & Artists members, I organized readings for those who were ready to read in public. Families and friends came to the Longmeadow Town Hall on the green for the readings, confirming for the writers an appreciation for their writing by a wider audience.

That year it was also time for Stephen to move to Florida, and I knew that I would go with him. Facing the writers' disappointment, I gave workshops on how to lead a group using role-playing, at which they learned that facilitating is not as easy as it appears. But these were accomplished writers who formed a new group, drawing in members from my groups plus new writers who continued to meet for about eight years.

For my last day with the young writers, I placed every specially chosen object from my significant shell collection from Cape Cod and Florida of conchs, welks, scallops, dark blue mussels, white angel wings, horseshoe crabs, beach glass, as well as treasured stones, pine cones bigger than their hands could circle, and other various items on my dining room table, fully covering it, and then, giving each a market paper bag, let them circle the table to choose one each time (each eyeing something hoped for) until all were gone.

Then on my final night, I invited the young writers to join the adult group, knowing what was going to happen. To the amazement of the older writers, the young writers gave accurate and appropriate responses to the older writers' work and produced excellent writing that left the older writers rapidly adjusting and responding just as they normally would and without regard to age (or the short height of the guest members!). I felt so proud to be able to have found a way to show the young writers that differences in age and education have nothing to do with being an accomplished writer.

Pat, with national and international accomplishments, for years, still graciously took the time to write as a close friend, as my most important woman mentor, and as one writer honoring another. To meet her, to watch her was to see a woman you'd say was kind and caring, smiled easily, and laughed at her mistakes. To assess her for her impact on giving a voice to the full spectrum of our population would require a tool that measures change created on a global scale.

RIPENING

You're my tall daughter. You tower over me
like the front maple grown higher than our home.
At eighteen you still come with questions: How
much lemon? Do I think this girl's
sexually abused? Will I go with you for fabric
for the senior prom—
it's more than money you want.

You're my ripening fruit whose laughter
thumps down stairs like spilled peaches.
You like your long, banana-yellow hair.
Some days you dress like a dog
so men won't notice you.
For years I didn't see your teeth—braces,
shyness, confusion, anger.
Of late the air between us tastes sweet.
Your smile has the whiteness of peeled apple.

It's late at night when I get home.
I see your bedroom window, a lighthouse
in the small, dark world of our home,
our yard under a few stars.
Will I come up? Your voice, low flute notes,
slips under the yellow crack of your door.
I'm the meal you didn't eat for years.
Now I'm the fruit you choose. I've peeled off
our past. I like being savored.

PJC 1992

CHAPTER 9

Discovering My Mother

When she became my Angel

Love has to spring spontaneously from within...[1]
Meher Baba

My mother grew up in Maine on a farm set between two small towns on a county road in North Newport, with a best friend her age at the only other farm visible from her farm, across a cow pasture. Naturally talented and accomplished at piano and cello, during her high school years she boarded in town and took elocution lessons from which she graduated to giving poetry recitations. At Farmington State Teachers College, studying for elementary school teacher certification, she played cello in the orchestra, was a member of the debating team, and showed us by her expression how proud she had been to always receive the highest mark for how she spoke, then added "and the lowest mark for what I said." One year a newsreel featured her as the Maple Syrup Queen of the State of Maine, brown eyes and hair curled in that year's longer style, with a smile deepening her dimple.

In our family life, she didn't perform in public, as her mother had in plays, but at home she enunciated her words and spoke with expression. With a flair for the dramatic that she displayed on occasion, in her forties she took up belly dancing, and we were her audience in the living room watching her gyrating hips jingling bells on a belt at the top of a long skirt and her spangled top glinting.

After she graduated from Farmington in 1938, having rejected a suitor, she taught for three years in a one-room schoolhouse, where, if the morning was freezing, she broke ice in the classroom water bucket. Isolated in the woods from all but the children and the family she boarded with, in bed she listened to the sounds of owls and train whistles screeching loudly and insistently through nights deep as a well.

Summers, my mother returned to the farm and waitressed. Pretty and popular with the local young men, she liked having a good time at dances and at county fairs with trotter races. In one photo she wore a hat with a feather at a jaunty angle. When we would ask her where she went to church, she'd say "the Methodist" to see if the new minister was good-looking. She was replacing the regular waitress at the inn in Corinna the night my father came in, 6 ft. 4¾ in. and handsome in a white dinner jacket, wearing a Duke University ring of gold, raised around a midnight blue stone, and on temporary assignment as production engineer at the Birds Eye pea-packing plant. She took his order. A year later, she opened his letter asking her to marry him, and on July 20th, 1941, Rowena Helen Titcomb and Wellington Morley Cramer III were married, honeymooning at Ripogenus Dam in the Maine north woods.

In a summer photo of 1945, I am two years old, with fine hair in a long wispy cap, looking at the camera from inside a small yard enclosed by a white picket fence, where my mother and I stand wearing matching white pinafore dresses with red rickrack. She is wearing spectator pumps. In a winter photo from that same year, my father holds me aloft with an angora hat tied under my chin as he smiles from a snowy Rochester sidewalk. As a girl I felt closer to him. I wanted to be in the yard where he was. And most likely that day, my mother was in the house, cleaning.

When I had to help my mother clean, it was with the dusting. The cloth felt dry in my hand and dust had to be repeatedly shaken off outside. In the living room I'd do the easy end tables, the Boston rocker with its tedious spokes and curved legs, and then the standing radio. It once had an antique soup tureen with a large platter behind it on top—until the day I ran through and the vibrations caused it to slide to the floor. Blamed for the irreplaceable loss, I was sent to my bedroom where unhappily, I sat behind the closed door knowing I'd been unfairly treated.

What I didn't mind was polishing the dining room table, rubbing circles of lemon oil over the curly grain, and across the top of the hunt board beneath the big, framed print of red-coated men on horseback ready for the chase, or lining up polished silverware on green velveteen in the hunt board drawer. Mechanically

I vacuumed, all the while waiting for the relief of being outdoors where I could breathe in the airy, shadowy under-spaces of oak and maple trees and feel free.

My view of my mother changed dramatically in 1991 when, at forty-eight, in my early years of spiritual searching, I discovered a new reason for respect and loyalty. One afternoon, with people I had met for the first time (except for Stephen, who I was with), I sat silently absorbed as a woman's voice, calm as a quiet fountain of words, took us up a golden staircase where at the top I would meet my golden angel. I knew little about angels and this was my first awareness there could be one who was mine. I restrained my curiosity of what this angel would look like, pausing at each step of the directions. When at last I reached the top and with great anticipation looked, hoping to see an angel, I was startled to see my mother standing there. My mother was my golden angel? My amazement felt immeasurable. My heart began to soften, and with the humility of new understanding, I knew that she had always loved me and loved me now; yet as a child unable to tell her, I hadn't felt as loved as I wanted. Having known my father as the more important parent, I saw my mother with new appreciation as my spiritual teacher. With a synchronicity I later called the "Divine Plan," I remembered in startling clarity the words that she had spoken (and perhaps to herself) nearly twenty years before, when she had said aloud, "I love myself." My mother was the first source of my knowing that to love myself was to love God. Years later, this truth became the way in which I celebrated her at her Remembrance service.

Around 1982, one summer morning, I arrived early at her Rhode Island home to go to Cape Cod for the day. She loved the beach, going barefoot on sand, the sun baking her skin, the waves rolling and dragging shells and seaweeds, all mingling with children's voices and crying gulls. We'd buy her iced black coffee there. On this day, before we left, I watched my father click a pouch around her waist—still able to care for her at home. I had come to have fun with her and give him a day for himself.

FACING EARLY ALZHEIMER'S

It is our annual visit to Cape Cod. My mother wears
a zippered pouch around her waist, where my father
has put her wallet, sunglasses, and a wet washcloth in
a plastic bag. He shows me the sixty dollars that is there,
telling me she is to wear the pouch so nothing gets
lost—and I know he means her.

From the passenger seat, she's her own radio station:
her memory changing like New England weather.
Wait a minute, and she tells a different story—like the
one about dating musicians, who weren't good dancers
because they were always thinking of the next note.

She's a strong woman, able to say she regretted some
decisions, like the loss of her BMW, bought for her in
her sixties. She drove that car everywhere—from Rhode
Island to Maine, to visit her mother, and to Reading,
where she'd lived most of her life. The day it was sold
for a bigger car so as not to lose its value, she didn't say
no, but after that she didn't drive much. I tell her to sell
BMWs in her next life, and we laugh, and to give one to
each of her grandchildren, and we keep on laughing.
Once, she reaches over and puts her open hand on the
back of my neck.

The forecast is for rain, but the sun comes out. I drive
through weeks and months of not being with her—and
now she is as close as the sweet iced tea I sip.
Her face is a maze of wrinkles where I couldn't find
a beginning from an end; her gray hair shines—
like light on metal—in glistening rain.

PJC   1982

CHAPTER 10

Discovering My Father

When I received "Staten Island Ferry-Boat"[1]

Most people are content with just the daily affairs of
life, but you and I are different. We've been given a
gift that is rare in this world, the gift of understanding, of seeing deep into the heart of things.... Learn
to use your gift...to question and see things that
no one else but you can, then write about what you
have learned. For only in giving back will you find
fulfillment.[2]

Ben Ericson

My father grew up in Brooklyn, New York. After his father left the family, he needed to help support his mother and two younger sisters in the pressing needs of the Great Depression of the 1930s. What I most remembered about the stories of his youth was that he went to Brooklyn Technical High School and read many books in the borough libraries. When he left Brooklyn it was for Duke University in North Carolina and a degree in mechanical engineering. I remember only a few details. I know he was proud to have met Captain Eddie Rickenbacker, a decorated hero of WW I. I heard, too, with his seemingly mild embarrassment, that he had participated with a group sitting around a table attempting to levitate it—and perhaps they had. What I loved hearing most though was when in a softened, nostalgic voice he recalled driving on balmy nights in Georgia under trees with hanging moss. Many years later I was driving north through the small towns in Georgia and found the road often close to front yards with old magnolias. I had slowed for a better look at the Spanish moss and felt a desire to stop and stay, but my journey was from Florida to New England, and I had to keep on heading north.

My father was a thinker as an engineering student, and a romantic as a nature poet enraptured by Spanish moss; those two abilities came together at his first purchased home in 1945 when I was two and my sister's birth anticipated. It was my father's ideas and hands that papered walls and created the tended gardens that made the strong, unforgettable views of my home. On a quiet street in Reading, he had found a colonial house where he made lovely rooms from his imagination, with windows that opened to beautiful views over a third of an acre of nature that his hands patiently shaped with the lawn mower and garden tools, fulfilling his desire for a verdant, private yard of his own.

My father's abilities had not come from his maternal grandfather, a man descended from Swedish coal miners. Instead, he had inherited them from Mr. Svenson, the man who had fathered his maternal grandmother's daughter Hilda Elizabeth, my father's mother, my grandmother, born out of wedlock. My father's gift of working with his hands and his deep enjoyment to do so he knew as his inheritance from his grandfather. He had cared that we knew how pleased he was to have Mr. Svenson as his true grandfather as Mr. Svenson had been a carpenter. I grew up standing with my "tall dad" at his high basement workbench built higher than my waist. Spending hours with him I learned how to hammer a nail, tighten a piece of scrap wood in the red vise, and saw.

On Saturday mornings I wanted to be in the yard where he was. He taught me to run the power mower, and I could pull out the choke, hold the handlebar in my left hand, and whip back the cord to make the engine roar. Happy behind the powerful throbbing, I steered with fourth-grade determination to the front yard first, where the thinner grass, although not interesting, was easiest to mow. Done there, I swung the mower to the denser grass off the porch, slowly approaching the back yard that was the hardest and best of all. Here the grass was thicker, darker green, and beautiful, growing down the hill to where it again became ordinary. I crisscrossed the hill, my arms tiring from steering and absorbing the vibrations, feeling proud, as, under the blades, neat, parallel cutting-lines dwindled shaggy grass. A rich odor hung in the air and my sneakers grew a half-coat of chlorophyll-green. That same year I'd be out in our driveway standing opposite him, far enough apart so he could toss me a ball as he repeated, "Keep your eyes on the ball." He believed girls needed to learn to catch. And I did.

What wasn't fun was my mother's assigning my spanking to him when I talked back. Her words, "Go to you room and wait until your father gets home," trailed behind me as I climbed the stairs past the white wainscoting and colonial wallpaper of large, red, vining flowers. Sitting on the edge of my bed, my dread increasing, I stared at my door with my name Barbara in small, white wooden script and listened as his size thirteen shoes thumped up the stairs. But by my teen years, he was the one who made standing up straight important in facing life. I'd feel his hands on my shoulders straightening them when I was slouching and hear, "Stick out your chest." His advice has held.

Then there were the years when my relations with my dad (and my mother) were not smooth. I was called a problem as a baby. Even my dad, my counselor of comfort through the swinging emotions of my high school and university years, let me know that at the time of my marriage he still held that view. The only change was that now, "I was my husband's problem." At forty-eight, with the beginning presence of spirituality in my life, I made an adjustment that ended that labeling. Then the following years of my increasing spiritual awareness brought more change that culminated in an astonishing reunion for us at eighty-eight and sixty-three. I heard his words of pride for me as the warmth of the sun bringing us back together.

I don't know when my father first started writing, but my guess is the 1970s. When he finally did share his writing with me, telling me that he mostly wrote at ten thousand feet on business trips to Europe, one typed piece was so special that I brought it to India, leaving behind a small collection of his narratives in Florida. The paper has a silhouette of the Staten Island ferry-boat on a crossing from Brooklyn to St. George. I can see, smell, hear, and feel what my dad did riding that ferry. As a man of his time who provided for his family, went out to dinner with his wife, and entertained their friends at home, a man who took pleasure in caring for our home and yard, he certainly wouldn't have ever wanted to take the time to join a writers' group. But he did just that in his assisted-living housing in his eighties, in a group with a writing facilitator where he gathered a following appreciative of his stories. And by eighty-eight, his mind still retained the energy to explore historical people and places through books.

He wouldn't live to see his writing published, but "A Raindrop Travelogue" and other stories have been in my blog. Here is my favorite poem of his, "Staten Island Ferry-Boat." I smile each time I read it, appreciative of his writing genes in me, just as my father was appreciative of his grandfather's carpentry genes in him.

STATEN ISLAND FERRY-BOAT

Most of my dreams, and I have had millions, seem best
to present themselves on the Staten Island Ferry-boat as
it ploughed its way from 69th Street in Brooklyn to St.
George on Staten Island. My mother was a dreamer—
mostly removing herself from reality. My dreams took
me all over the world, all over the United States. They
took me there in balloons, on trains, and on camel back.
I was very much taken with Richard Halliburton and
his Royal Road to Romance. He rode a bicycle around
the pyramids, he pranced through the Taj Mahal, and
he swam the Hellespont. I was a great lover of Lawrence
of Arabia. Funny how I have always had such an affinity
for the Germans and the Arabs. Have you ever smelled
the water in the Narrows between Brooklyn and Staten
Island? Have you ever smelled hemp from a tramp
steamer lying at its dock? Have you ever smelled a
coffee roaster riding on the Sea Beach Express over
the Manhattan Bridge? Can you possibly imagine the
aroma in Bridgeton, N.J. at the Ritter plant in
Catsup-making time? Can you feel the aroma of tar
and coal oil as it is freshly laid on a dusty road? I can
even smell snow and rain.

WMC c 1970s

MY FATHER'S TOMATOES

Staked in pungent mulch,
the jungly tomato vines rose
serpentine with calyx crowns.
Hard green tomatoes hung
beneath heated leaves.
Roots reached into compost:
past Easter eggshells,
morning coffee grounds,
peach skins, and lettuce dung.
Lured by sun and rain
and father's visits, tomatoes
inflated. Grinning
he brought them to the kitchen,
savory odor clinging to his clothes.

PJC   1985

AWAKENING

CHAPTER II

"Always Loved"

1987–1991

You are so much more than I ever expected, so much more
than I thought I deserved. I see God in your face and God
in your grace, and love makes its home in your heart.[1]

Stephen Michael Camp

Stephen and I first met at an advertising company in Connecticut in 1987 where I had been a paste-up artist for six years. He had moved from New Mexico to become the new department manager. I liked him, but that would be brief. The morning I overheard him talking about his personal life, as my drawing board was in front of his office, I realized that our values were quite different, and my respect ended. Two months later, just before Christmas, he fired all part-timers, of which I was one, and disbelieving, I asked to see him. But the staff member who had brought the message told me that Stephen had refused, reinforcing my previously formed opinion of him. By the time I reached my car, I noticed that my regret over the firing was gone, and I actually felt relieved.

Over the next two years, I saw him only twice—once briefly passing in nearby Northampton, Massachusetts where we recognized each other but didn't speak, then a second time when hearing someone at my back door and forgetting I was in a slip, I entered the kitchen to see a Darth Vader image behind the screen door, quickly turned, and came back dressed. It was Stephen. He was in his cycling outfit—black Lycra jersey and knee pants, and still wearing his black helmet. He asked to rent a summer cottage that I owned.

In 1988, Beth graduated from Rhode Island University. Megan, in high school, slept with her cat, Mellow, on the second floor where a young red maple reached toward the window of her small bedroom. Across the hall was her art room. Since Paul had moved out, my bedroom had been in a former study in the back extension of the house where the protecting branches of rhododendrons covered the lower part of two windows facing east and west. The full mirror that faced my bed had affirmations taped around its edges. But by May 1990, I had removed the affirmations and stopped taking antidepressants on my own. In June, as I was washing dishes and daydreaming, looking through a newly-leafed maple at a sky of the palest blues and peach, I suddenly heard the words, "my cup runneth over." Gently startled, I looked around. I had no knowledge of what an inner voice was, but no one was with me. I had felt comforted with the thought that this must mean I was doing fine.

Referred to a massage therapist in East Longmeadow, I phoned her office. During our call, she asked if I knew I was obsessing; I had answered yes. She asked me to meet with her. As I sat on a chair facing her, she had pounded my thighs, repeating, "You are out of your body." When she stopped she told me that I needed to become grounded. She told me that a spiritual study group met on the second floor of the two-story, gray, wood-frame building. At her suggestion, I agreed to go to a meeting.

On my second night at *A Course in Miracles*, I kept glancing, unnoticed I hoped, at a man across from me who I couldn't place. Thinking that he might be one of my daughters' former teachers and wanting to be polite, I had said hello, introducing myself and waiting to have my memory jogged. Instead, it was Stephen. Losing my composure, I excused myself and going down the stairs beside Judy Ebeling, one of our leaders, I told her of my experience with him, to which she smiled and said, "Your paths are probably meant to cross." I drove home baffled.

During that same week, I had an opportunity to see how I had already benefited from the group, using one of the first lessons I learned. Beth had come through the front door directing her anger at me standing in the dining room, and as her feet took the stairs by force, watching, without moving, I was able to keep my mouth closed. With the sound of her door slamming, I had whispered, "She certainly isn't extending love. She must need love." Feeling amused by my ability to remain silent, my smile widened, and my body relaxed. For the first time, I had successfully read her real need and respected her, rather than reacting and attempting to resolve her behavior.

At the third meeting, Stephen had announced that he was di-
vorced and had been fired from his position, bought off by a year's
work as a company courier. Even knowing this, I continued sitting
as far away from him as possible, yet each night a pattern repeated
itself. I would ask a question about how to apply the lesson to one
of my family situations, but no one would speak. Finally, Judy
would turn to Stephen who each time referred to certain lines,
explained them in words I could understand, and then returned
his attention to the book. I went home feeling helped and began
looking each week to where he sat when I asked my question.

I was the only one asking personal questions, but I didn't let
that deter me for I wanted to know what *A Course in Miracles*
had to do with me at that point in my life—what new thought
I might glean that I could carry home weekly and use to be a
better parent. Not until many years later did I find validation for
my questioning when reading mythologist Joseph Campbell's
views on his years of teaching in the 1960s at Sarah Lawrence, an
all-women's college. "At that college not only did we follow the
interests of the students, we found out what the interests were....
I was forced by my female students to consider the material from
the point of view of the woman.... 'What does the material mean
to life? What does it mean to me? I don't care why this myth occurred there, and then over there, but not over here. What does it
mean to me?'"[2] I had wanted to know what *A Course in Miracles*
meant from a mother's point of view.

One night in October I felt an inner change and stayed after the
meeting to hear Stephen sing, something that he did that I had
avoided. I was still seated when he had put away his guitar, and for
a second time I heard an inner voice. This time the message was,
"I like you." I protested. I was not going to say this, knowing immediately the words were for Stephen, and I found myself physically unable to stand. As my resistance lessened, I gripped my
courage and went to where he sat talking with a woman. Reach-

ing down, I lightly touched his arm, said the words, and started to straighten. Suddenly, instead of being the only one upright, I found myself tightly wrapped in his arms, looking up at him as he said, "I have always loved you and have been waiting for you to figure it out." My reaction was swift, startled, and confused. I disengaged from his arms and went to the stairs, aware that I had to pay attention to get down safely. For a year and a half I had succeeded in having no men in my life. Yet, to my amazement, in the car, a small thrill began moving through me. I liked it.

The following Friday, he asked me out for dinner at La Cazuela in Northampton. I'd been at a Unitarian Church meeting for eight hours and my response to him was that I was going to clean my bathroom that weekend. It was November. I added I had plans for Christmas. But I would appreciate a rain check. Later he told me that he had thought I wasn't interested, and I let him know my rain check had been a big accomplishment, as I'd first felt scared, then pleased. He told me he'd felt scared, too. At the group's first meeting in January, I told him that if he'd like to stop by my home on the way to his place, I would enjoy hearing a few songs. When I got home, I built a fire and wondered, until I heard his car pull up. I learned then that his long-ago comments in the office that I had found so upsetting had been made in jest. And that he had been in love with me when he fired me and that was why he couldn't face me that day.

Stephen's willingness to share his love and my readiness to date after being on my own for a year and a half resulted in a budding friendship, nurtured within the familiarity of a group of people engaged in spiritual studies. Unbeknown to us was that I was on the verge of facing occult experiences that Stephen, due to his own experiences, would understand and support.

What I also didn't know until much later was that Meher Baba was there supporting me as well. In April 1995, during one of Stephen's private toning sessions, I received channeled information for one of Stephen's clients. It was a powerful message of the true nature of love. And although the message might have had some relevance for the client, I knew that it was a message for me. I just didn't know that it was from Meher Baba, who had yet to enter my life in a conscious way. Looking back, I see that the clue was there—as for this one and only time in my work, the information did not come to me in my own voice, but rather through a voice that identified itself.

> The principle of love is one we are to integrate into our lives beginning with the first breath and ending with the last at which time we are to remember the energy whereof we are from and release ourselves into the gentle embrace of the one energy who divined us.[3]
>
> *Aurora*

CHAPTER 12

Early Occult Experiences

1990–1992

While the aspirant is experiencing psychic unfoldment,
occasional manifestations of the subtle world will come
to him in the form of significant visions, light, colors,
sounds, odors, bodiless journeys, and contacts.... Occult
experiences are vouchsafed the aspirant only when abso-
lutely necessary for his spiritual development.[1]

Meher Baba

It was after I had joined *A Course in Miracles* that one night, sitting on the edge of my bed and reading a few pages in a book on meditation without much understanding, I found a phrase suggested for practice, and began my routine of repeating "neti neti" (not this, not that). After several nights something unusual happened. As I watched, above the bedroom lamp, on the dimly lit ceiling, yellow light was creating different patterns. Having no idea what it was, I said, "There's yellow energy moving on the ceiling" without knowing what I meant, thought it interesting, and fell asleep. Telling no one, I watched nightly for it to reappear. I had had two experiences before, spaced years apart, which I now understand as individual appearances of my occult ability. But this one I consider to be the significant beginning.

Soon after this, on my way to Amherst to a Thursday evening writing workshop, I saw purple light moving along the field side of the highway. Not wanting a ticket, I turned to see how close the police were and found no car. Yet the light reappeared weekly at a certain spot.

In February, Stephen introduced me to Hope Community Church, where he had begun to sing. I learned that its worship was based on *A Course in Miracles*, and so I, too, began attending services there. Now I was traveling to Amherst every Sunday from my home in Longmeadow. Returning home one morning, on the same highway where I had earlier seen the purple light, I noticed green light moving back and forth across the dashboard. Then at the same place the following Sunday, the sun and sky turned pink. My unassuming thought was that I must be seeing the invisible light spectrum.

Soon after, I painted a watercolor rainbow and in ink made a simple outline of a young girl, naked, climbing it; then when I heard words and melodies for two simple songs to God, I sang them each night as lullabies.

In a succession of weeks, different inner visions appeared. Between wakefulness and sleep, I saw American Indians. Men on horseback wore long headdresses, or a single black and white feather tied upside down. They pulled travois toward a village of tents. A pillar of white fire rose beside my bed, from where Jesus looked out, and I went in and out of the flames, not feeling heat. I heard three names—Meshach, Shadrach, and Abednago—that I recognized but had to look up to discover that they were mentioned in the Bible.

In a vision that grew longer and fuller each night, I walked at the edge of a field and then into a forest, accompanied by a growing number of animals—first a fawn, then a rabbit, a snake, and more. Where I turned, a fat, dusty-golden mare stood with her head up, or sometimes grazing. Near the mare, a snow fence appeared that was keeping back *Where the Wild Things Are* monsters who were crying from behind wooden slats, "We'll eat you up—we love you so!"[2] Beside them stood an Appaloosa horse, head up, never grazing, who I knew was my protector. When I saw a plastic Appaloosa in a secondhand store window, I brought it home for my bedside table, where I kept it for two years.

In the forest, I stood with the animals in a glade bright with sun. It had a rectangle of earth for a garden, where Jesus first appeared wearing a white turtleneck jersey, planting seeds. Later, he hovered once above me, in a white robe ablaze in light. Emerging from the forest, I rode my dusty-golden mare bareback, galloping along a country lane through an apple orchard, then up into the blue sky.

I had no knowledge of Stephen's occult experiences until I shared my visions with him. Now I learned that he had been to The Light Institute in Galisteo, New Mexico, and he mentioned Chris Griscom, both of which at the time meant nothing to me; I wasn't even aware of what the land of New Mexico looked like. Since then I have discovered that Chris Griscom established The Light Institute in 1985, following which she became globally recognized as a spiritual healer and teacher.

Years later, when Meher Baba entered my life, I had found an explanation for my visions in *Silent Teaching of Meher Baba*. Now understanding that my experiences were for my spiritual development, I continued reading and discovered the following, "While occult phenomena often play an important role in the re-generation of the aspirant, it is essential for him to be aware that, no matter how real they seem, they are no less the product of false imagination than the ordinary phenomena of the gross world."[3]

Stephen was the only one I told. He listened but didn't make any comments beyond affirming my experiences while sharing his own, providing a space of acceptance for me. At a non-verbal level, I sensed that he was an anchor of safety for me.

GOD IS GOOD *Song*

God is good,
God is in me,
God is in everyone,
Every path leads to God.

PJC 1990

HEART OF GOD *Song*

I live in the heart of God,
I love in the heart of God,
I grow in the heart of God,
His heart is my real home.

God's heart is filled with Love
that I may know His Light.
I am the Love of God;
I am the Light.

PJC 1990

CHAPTER 13

The Seeds of India

1954 *AND* 1956
1979 *AND* 1992
When you become Mine,
Then you will find that
I am already yours.[1]

Meher Baba

I once said that I would never live in Florida nor go to India, but by my early fifties I had done both. When I asked, "When did India appear in my life?" the seeds I uncovered surprised me, with the final seed being for Stephen as well as for me.

I became aware of the planting of the first seed of India when writing this book. It came about when I was eleven. My paternal grandfather owned an estate in Cohassett, on the south shore of Boston, where, in the fifth grade, I went with my family for the big celebration of my great-grandparents' 50th wedding anniversary. After eating ice cream cake, I wandered away from the adult talk and explored the sunroom with its thirteen grandfather clocks, the marble stairs, the lengthy, second-floor hall of bedrooms, and the sloping lawn with beehives in back that ended at a seawall. I stopped a long time in front of a big glass case of carved elephants, each one different in size or material or pose, and wondered why anyone would collect them. Elephants were far away from my world. That visit was the last time I saw my grandfather, and I didn't get to ask about the elephants. Now I remembered his. In India I had one small, red elephant carving with the trunk raised in the most auspicious pose, which stood beside my special photos for good fortune.

The second seed was a childhood purchase in Corinna, the town near my maternal grandparents' farm in Maine. Across from the mill, with its machinery that we heard clanking through big, open windows, were small shops. One day, at about age thirteen, carrying money in my wallet, I walked by, searching for the record shop, and left with a "Big Band" LP for my boxy turntable at home. Listening to "Begin the Beguine," I especially liked the parts where the saxophones sounded like a flock of flamingos lifting up, gliding, then landing. When in 2003, I moved to Meherabad, Meher Baba's Tomb-Shrine in India, I heard "Begin the Beguine" every year as it was one of Meher Baba's favorite songs.

I didn't find another seed until my mid-thirties, but this one was specific to India. Taking acting classes at New York's HB Studio (Herbert Berghof Studio), one of my teachers casually told me of a woman he knew who had gone to India searching for... and then he had paused and added, "I don't know what," with a little shrug and a smile, as if there were nothing worthwhile to be found in India. I had known then that India was definitely a place that I did not want to go.

There would be one more seed. In 1992, returning home on the Massachusetts Turnpike on a warm afternoon, Stephen and I pulled into a rest stop. When I started to get out of the passenger side of the car, my back unexpectedly hurt. Suddenly, I could barely move, as if my mind and body had become disconnected. Stephen had to open the door for me. I headed slowly toward the women's room inside the big lobby, but instead found myself well inside the men's room with no awareness of how I got there. Dazed and scared, I turned back. Nothing like this had ever happened before.

Once home, I lay on the floor and cried. I had never been to a chiropractor, but calling a new friend from the floor's support, I garbled my need until my tears ended when I heard her assurance that she went to an excellent one. I made my appointment. At forty-nine, I considered myself to be in good physical condition. All I could identify as the source of my pain was a simple job of carrying a heavy bag of books into Hope Community Church from my car a few hours before the trip. The real reason came as an insight when I was ready to believe what would have been too unusual for my sensibilities as I lay prone on the floor that day.

This doctor introduced me to new ways of treatment that were transformational, combining traditional practice with the use of energy. I was intrigued and agreed to wear a crystal. As I was lying on her table one day, she asked me when I had begun wearing glasses. I easily remembered. It was in 1955. I was in seventh grade. In math class, fourth seat in the row closest to the door, sudden blinding flashes of light across my field of vision scared me, so I raised my hand to ask to go to the girls' room. I decided to have the office call my mother. The eye doctor said I needed glasses for far-sightedness, but had no explanation for the lightning, as I thought of it, which hadn't returned. I had picked out light blue frames.

The response from the chiropractor was different. She said we begin wearing glasses when we can no longer bear to see the world as it appears to us. Moving from the role of doctor for me and for Stephen, she became a friend, and in time, a spiritual guide who shared her spiritual teacher in India. "You need to go to India" would be her future words. By then I had already been seeing visions, so the day she spoke of India I told her I was seeing something humorous about Stephen, whom she was at that moment treating. He was up a tree, frightened by sheep at the bottom bleating "bah bah." Turning to me smiling, she laughed and said emphatically, "'Baba' is the Indian word for father, or teacher," thus the final seed and the reason for the experience of my back pain.

1955
ROBERT COOTEY

I have forgotten the name of my seventh-grade
homeroom teacher, but not that of Robert Cootey.
Considered pretty and smart, I was doomed to hear
Robert's bad jokes and offhand remarks
about my grades—as his soft, clumsy hands
collapsed on the green library table we shared.
I had the long side. Robert had the end.
Clear as a Polaroid photo, I remember the teacher—
a slight woman whose boxy suit jacket fell in
on her chest.
I wasn't fooled by her phony smile.
Her humor was to call us by our last names first,
so his always got a laugh as she crooned,
"Cootey, Robert."
"Young, John," made us nod approval
while my name didn't get a rise.
I felt sorry for Robert whose grades
were no better than the brunt of her teasing.
Good grades, nice clothes, and a big house
were how I measured people then.
The teacher wore open-toe, crepe wedge sandals
over reinforced-toe stockings—eliminating her
from my imagination;
Robert chose the blandness of whites, beiges,
and muted plaids. Now that we're past fifty,
I hope he's President of his own company.
I remember he smiled a lot—which would probably
endear him to me now.
I hope his lumbering body—barely under control

then—has aged into trim, healthy ripeness—and if he has a family, let them appreciate that I endured a lot so Robert could grow up.

PJC 1990s

CHAPTER 14

Living in the Present

1993–1995

Trust no Future, howe'er pleasant!
Let the dead Past bury its dead!
Act,—act in the living Present!
Heart within, and God o'erhead![1]
Henry Wadsworth Longfellow

There is a kind of past that I experienced during the years with Stephen in which I remained aware of the present but would simultaneously be in a different time period. Although four of the regressions (as I considered them) between 1993 and 1995 caused terror when I was in them, I thought that each could be releasing remnants from those lives that were blocking my spiritual development.

The first experience began when Barbara Hero and Robert Foulkrod arrived at eleven p.m. one night at my home in Longmeadow, having driven from Gray, Maine, with the express purpose to meet Stephen. His voice had the tonal quality Barbara was looking for to use in experimenting with the Lambdoma Keyboard,[2] her invention (helped by engineers and a manufacturer) for healing through sound. Very soon after their visit, I accompanied Stephen to their home where we learned that Barbara was also a visual artist, composer, writer, and mathematician, and Robert, a revered researcher in spiritual awakening. Knowledgeable about the work of Phineas Quimby in the mid-1850s, Robert had directed Stephen to Quimby's theories of mentally aided healing, and Stephen left understanding not only the importance of the work of Barbara but also that of Phineas Quimby.

Sometime later, because of that visit, I returned to attend a workshop (Stephen had a commitment elsewhere) as Barbara was presenting Shaman Foster Perry, author of *When Lightning Strikes a Hummingbird: The Awakening of a Healer*,[3] whose story intrigued me. Seated in a workshop circle of fifty people, I was more alert to Foster's style of presentation than to my presence as a participant (by that time I'd had numerous healing experiences) when Foster loosely took my hand. He began speaking casually, saying that I was the subject of both medical experimentation in Atlantis and royal incest in Egypt, and suddenly I felt his now solid grip holding my weight as I slid, screaming, to the floor. Barbara afterwards described my face as "unrecognizable."

Within the next month, I met Foster privately when he told me of a "tumbril" (an open-backed, wooden cart) carrying my dead body, still dressed in priest robes, through the streets, and in inner vision, I saw in "brown-light" a wooden cart with big wheels passing through a square dimly lit by the dirty-gold downward rays of street lamps during the French Revolution and felt terror.

My third experience occurred at the Spanish-style Unity on the Bay in Miami where Stephen was giving an advanced sound healing workshop in the large library. He had stopped for a lunch break, going to the kitchen with others while I remained in the room, seated beside a man I didn't know. When the man casually asked what fire meant to me, I had begun telling him of raking leaves as a child, until he interrupted and said, "Six hundred years ago, fire..." at which point, I saw total blackness except for a blazing line of fire, and heard myself repeatedly scream, "Don't kill me, don't kill me, don't kill me." My eyes had closed, but I could feel people moving closer to help when suddenly Stephen's voice cut through the air as he rushed in, telling them not to touch me and that I knew what I was doing. Gripping his shirt, I hung on until uncurling my fingers he laid me on the floor. My voice continued, but I was feeling the exhaustion of the repetition of those words, then the words shortened to, "Don't kill, don't kill, don't kill," and as my energy was nearly spent, to, "Don't, don't, don't." Now quiet, I moved from lying prone to crawling in a wide circle, continuing to play out my escape. For forty minutes my consciousness stayed locked in the 1300s while I remained aware, although less so, of the library and people. Stephen had asked only once if I were through, and still feeling tension, although greatly diminished, I said no. As the regression came to its completion, I found myself in an animal shed in France where a farmer helped me—then I exited the time period and became aware of the present. Even though enervated, I felt calm and quiet. Almost everyone else had become agitated. Those who weren't stood behind those who were, hands on their shoulders as Stephen re-formed the group and asked the man who he was—"Lawrence Furman,"[4] he replied, "My guides told me to come here today," and pointing at me continued, "and that she was the lightning rod for others to go through their death knells." Each participant then told of his or her memories of death.

One other experience happened in 1994, after my experience in Florida. When we toured the Southwest, Stephen knew pure joy in Santa Fe, where, he said, he'd biked ten thousand miles. Having been in Sedona twice previously, on a tour of the Southwest with my daughter Megan and for a workshop for me, it was the joy of being among the red rock canyons again. One day we climbed to the glass-enclosed Chapel of the Holy Cross in Sedona, and as I walked down the aisle, I glanced to my right, saw a picture of Jesus, and then looked away. Feeling my gaze drawn back, I turned my face and was again looking over my right shoulder. As I kept moving, I suddenly lost strength, erupting in sobs of fear that racked my body. I entered a pew and gripped the wooden back, sinking to my knees. There were heavy hoofbeats of horses but all I could see were the stirrups attached to the saddles, and the men's muscular calves laced with leather thongs. I was in a pit, in a brown monk's robe, being pelted by stones. Then I saw Jesus, followed by his disciples, walking on a narrow trail to another destination. (My first editor explained that leather thongs were not worn in this time period, but my inner understanding was to report what I saw without adjustment.) Finally quieting, when I opened my eyes, I saw that Stephen had been crying too.

Later that year, Stephen and I, as guests at a sweat lodge in central Massachusetts, had sat off to the side of a farmhouse living room where people were tightly packed in rows of chairs. When the owner stood to say he had messages to deliver first, I didn't understand that he meant channeling. After several, he described me not by name but by information that only I could recognize at that moment, saying "There is an old Indian woman who would like to work with you."

Afterwards, during the sweat lodge, I had a sudden glimpse of the battle of Wounded Knee, causing me to leave that day thinking that the message for me had been from an American Indian. I thought, "Corn Woman?"

Three years later, though, in Pune, India, while visiting the shrine of Muslim Perfect Master Hazrat Babajan for the first time, I heard a message from her. It was then I understood that she was the old Indian woman who had spoken to me through the farm owner's voice. Eventually I read that Perfect Masters do not speak at their places of pilgrimage, but I believe in the constancy of Babajan's messages, and not what I read. On one occasion her words were so hard to accept that I immediately and vehemently denied them, saying, "I am not...!" and for the next six months lived with leg pain so strong that I could barely walk. I had landed hard on my seat when the bus back to Meherabad went over a bump. But I knew in my heart that the true cause was my blatant disobedience to Babajan. While I felt a deep familiarity with her and held her in fondness, I had overstepped her boundary for me. On my next visit to her shrine, I lay my forehead on her body cloth, my outstretched hand open with a flower, and carefully repeated her earlier words, accepting them.

When I found validation of past lives in *God Speaks* by Meher Baba described as "a minutely detailed description of the journey of the soul..."[5] I accepted that for purposes of my spiritual growth in this lifetime, I had been taken to past lives to know that I was more than my present body and in truth that I am an eternal soul.

It was June when Stephen and I left Western Massachusetts for mid-central Maine to visit my grandparents' gravestones by a route that took us farther east to camp in Acadia National Park and then to Machiasport near the most eastern point of the United States. We drove to the end of a long row of isolated houses that faced only the cold, blue Atlantic and a sardine factory. Elizabeth, one of my mother's closest friends, knew we were coming. Listening to her stories brought back my mother as a younger woman, as seen through Elizabeth's eyes, and I left with the warmth of her memories.

My excitement began to rise when we turned into the curved drive of my grandparents' farm. Edging to the front of my seat, ready, I got out, went up the porch steps and knocked. The owners, while surprised, seemed pleased to see us. When they offered us a tour, Stephen took out his camera. But the more I saw the more I was disappointed. The barn remained, but the tall, unfinished boards of the attic with its suitcases and hatboxes dusty in shafts of sunlight (one of my special places) had been renovated. A contemporary bedroom with a sliding glass door overlooked the field whose edges had filled my hands with wild strawberries. I left with unrealized hope but wiser.

Farther down the road, at the church to where the pony Beauty had pulled my mother's family, Stephen strummed his guitar and sang "Amazing Grace" on the 4th of July, one of only two dates a year that the church is open. It was a rare moment to be recognized as Rowena Titcomb's daughter, sitting where my mother had as a child. After the service, mingling out front with the Smith family who'd known me when I was young, one son asked where I was based, and without thinking, what came out was, "In God," startling us both into staring at one another, speechless. And then I sat by my grandparents' gravestones, the need that I had come to fulfill.

By returning to the places of my past, I have given my memories a home in my writing, discovering there a new appreciation. Yet there is another aspect to this. My past lives better in my writing, and I live better in the present, a truth I found in Longfellow's "The Psalm of Life," and also in Stephen's "You Can't Go Back,"

"You can visit but you can't go back...Your past is just as cold as
ice...Everything is perfect living in the present where your spirit
is the best guide in town."[6] Stephen's words and those of Longfellow came together with these words of Meher Baba's in *The
Everything and the Nothing*, "Live more and more in the present
which is ever beautiful and stretches away beyond the limits of
the past and future."[7] I had been taken to past lives to know that
I was more than my present body, and by my own experience in
this lifetime learned the importance of living "more and more"
in the present. From the truths of a poet, a songwriter, and the
God-Man, I am freer.

ACADIA

Talking pines look down
upon out tent. Earlier
as I read stars
you softly sang
beyond the campfire's flare,
strumming your guitar.

Tonight the ground is solid
scented, swept of stones
and twigs. Your warm breath
dances on my neck,
as embers' piney fragrance
enters dreams.

PJC 1993

CHAPTER 15

Love, Serve, Forgive

1991–1995

All that I am, all that I give,
Oh it's my reason, my reason to live,
In sweet surrender, sweet surrender
to the will of the Lord.[1]

Stephen Michael Camp

The way the morning sun strikes brightness to the New Mexico desert was how Stephen loved his motto, "Love, Serve, Forgive." It inspired his living and his performing. At sixteen, he had asked his father, "What is truth?" and been told there was none. As a young man, he'd hugged a tree and heard, "Knowing the truth is not a virtue, living it is." Now he had come to the place in his life where he could answer his own question, telling me that all he wanted was to sing his songs to God. He struck a chord of trust and knowing in me of new meaning for life.

One Sunday at Hope Community Church, guest minister Rev. Edwene Gaines[2] presented a workshop to the congregation entitled *The Four Spiritual Laws of Prosperity*. At one point she asked us to write down what we would like to receive in a week. Stephen wrote "a new guitar." When we left, he was sure he'd have one. The following Friday he arrived early at a client's office in eastern Massachusetts. Taking out his guitar (an old Martin), he sat by a pond and began restringing it, when a man stopped to question him. Telling his listener that he was a singer and the songs he wrote he sang only to God, he told him about the prosperity workshop and that he knew he would get that new guitar. Two days later, in front of the Hope congregation, Stephen held up his new Martin, relating how the man had said, "Come with me," and at his bank had withdrawn a thousand dollars. Stephen then closed his eyes (as usual) and played "Sweet Surrender"—his fingers swiftly strumming, his body following his voice, vibrating emotionally from faith and joy.

I followed Stephen into new experiences where he was already comfortable. There were different books to read and spiritual groups and workshops to go to. By the spring of 1992, he'd found work delivering advertising on foot to homes and, more lucratively, recording voice-overs where he met with success due to his resonant voice and his abilities with inflection and characterization. Because we were living together, he generously put most of his money toward household expenses.

Stephen first discovered vocal toning (sound healing) through researching the original discoverers. Joy Gardner describes it as "the sustained, vibratory sounding of single tones...without the use of melody, rhythm or words...—a valuable tool for spiritually awakening people."[3]

Stephen began experimenting with vocal toning on me. The first time he directed his voice to my seven energy centers (also known as chakras) beginning with the base of my spine, the phone rang as he reached the seventh, the crown of my head. He stopped to answer the call and immediately I felt light-headed, which I told him when he returned. He then began at the crown and gradually brought his voice back down. I was fine then. In that moment he knew he was a sound healer.

Researching to learn more, he discovered Jonathan Goldman, author of *Healing Sounds: The Power of Harmonics*,[4] founder of The Sound Healers Association and a global leader in the field, who writes that "vocal harmonics...[uses] the voice to create two notes at the same time," while "overtoning...[is] to project those harmonics to another person...[as] sacred sounds for healing another."[5] After taking a workshop with Jonathan in New Hampshire, and at Stephen's request, Jonathan was able to help activate Stephen's ability to create overtones in the manner of the Gyü-to Tantric Monks, and Stephen's proficiency developed. During the next three years, he used overtoning not only in formal healing sessions but also in healing performance. He distinguished himself with a "mystical whistling" using the raga scale, and in particular when overtoning the moving hymn "Amazing Grace," whose rounded, clear notes penetrated hearts.

As creative writing groups were meeting weekly at my home, Stephen, inspired to teach, started his own groups with those who had been in attendance at his presentations of "Vocal Wellness"—techniques for healing by using the voice—and had expressed strong interest in learning from him. Subsequently, he reached out to give workshops in two other states.

One night upon returning from a workshop in central Massachusetts, he told me that he had asked a volunteer to lie on the massage table and the group to surround him. "This is the body of Jesus," he said. (I still hold the effect on me when he told me those words.) Then he began "angel toning," his new awareness of how a natural, healing harmony was created from each participant vocalizing individual tones in a succession of continuing sound. This created a unique "song," not only altering the volunteer's inner awareness and promoting relaxation (I know this from my own participation as receiver and as one toning), but also joining the surrounding "angels" in healing oneness through the resulting near hypnotic, tonal vibrations.

We participated in each other's groups, and there, I began seeing inner images and hearing words at each of the energy centers of all of the other participants. I was extending beyond information about me to inner sight and inner hearing about another. When I saw a bear at the root chakra, it was the activity of the bear (a human behavior) that suggested an aspect of the person. At the mid-body I saw sunflowers and deer at the heart—a doe standing below a buck higher up suggested that a woman had a protector. I saw a typewriter at the throat, guides at the center of the forehead (third eye), and, later, scenes of abuse at the navel center. My information was apart from any knowledge that I had of the participant. Initially, I referred to this as "seeing pictures" and wrote them down in a notebook. As their regularity expanded, I heard, "There's an angel sitting on my head, and her name is Lucida." Buying a new notebook, I dedicated it to God, as I knew God was the source and I was His instrument.

Rev. Carlos Anderson of Hope Community Church had toured as a singer with his musician partner in Florida, and now he gave Stephen a letter of introduction to those Unity churches and encouraged him to tour. Having little money, we drove south in Stephen's 1965 navy blue Saab (restored by my son-in-law) carrying the names of people who would welcome our staying with them. In gratitude to Carlos for the opportunity he had opened, Stephen wrote "Teach Only Love:" "Carlos, I wrote this song for you, it's my gift of feathers and stones, to tell you that you're walking on the right path, to comfort you when you're all alone. And it's love, love, love, all you teach is love, love, love. Every time you stumble and you get back up, you show us all the way back home ..."⁵

Unity on the Bay in Miami was one of the churches on our first tour. Stephen was singing in the service and giving sound healing workshops, at which time I was able to give just brief readings. When I found *You Are Psychic!* in the bookstore, as I'd been looking for a way to have my abilities confirmed, I recognized that its author, Pete A. Sanders, Jr.,⁶ a Massachusetts Institute of Technology honors graduate with principal studies in bio-chemistry and brain science, was the one I wanted to study with. In order to attend any of his workshops, I had to pass an oral exam given by one of his instructors to test my psychic abilities. Of the four abilities possible, I had three that the instructor identified by a percentage: clairvoyance (clear seeing), omniscience (knowing by presence of a thought), and clairaudience (clear hearing); I did not have clairsentience (clear feeling). Now accepted, I signed up for a two-week workshop in Sedona at Free Soul, founded by Sanders in 1980. Remembering my trip there with Megan the year before, I felt excited to think that I could return.

In a group gathered from across the country, I benefited from practices with the senses beyond those five that are physical, using what Sanders calls our four Soul senses through which we receive invisible images, feelings, sounds, and knowing, all informing us. One night, at eleven o'clock, he took us up Oak Creek Canyon to watch as the day began at 12:01 a.m. For me this was a new and startling understanding of time (although in truth obvious if thought about) as I had always thought of day as starting in the hours of 5:00 to 6:00 a.m. Now after this second trip, with both simple experiences and more complex new experiences like this one, I returned with a clearer understanding of my abilities and increased self-confidence, due not only to the workshop, but also because of Sedona itself, a land of energy vortices amid red rock buttes that jut up above miles of sparse, gray-green juniper and pinion pine.

As Stephen added individual sessions in Vocal Wellness, I was able to offer longer readings in his sessions, then in my own, direct my voice to energy centers, rapidly writing down what was communicated to me. During this same time period, I also continued to offer writing workshops in the Amherst Writers & Artists' method, which I very much enjoyed, especially when one grateful participant told me, "I haven't written since I was in college when the professor told me that I wasn't Ernest Hemingway and shouldn't try to write like him!"

In August 1994, Stephen and I planned a trip to India to see our chiropractor's guru. At the last moment, Megan, who had wanted to come, but wasn't because I'd said that I couldn't justify the cost, went to her financial aid advisor who told her to go, which manifested a dream I had of Megan waving good-bye to us standing on the steps of the jet then standing beside us.

In Whitefield, we joined several thousand in the presence of revered guru Sathya Sai Baba,[7] with women and men seated separately. On different days, I touched the guru's feet, spoke to him, then handed him my poetry chapbook to sign, which he kept, causing me a few tears of wondrous surprise. A smiling woman devotee, misunderstanding, told me to be happy and I was.

Stephen spent time alone with Hari, a devotee who appeared to have chosen Stephen to talk to. Hari told Stephen, who relayed to me, not to hope for an interview with the guru, as it might be because a family member would be passing over. Megan spent most of her time reading and sleeping in a whitewashed cowshed we lived in, but once at home she made four major changes to her life.

With a return flight together not possible, Megan left two days before Stephen and I followed. When we were approaching New York, he began rapidly writing three songs, one of which was "Embodiment of Love (Prema Swarupa)" that I later realized was the inspiration for my future name.

Encouraged by our chiropractor, the following year the three of us again traveled together, this time across Massachusetts to wait seven hours and be among the last blessed, at midnight, by Mata Amritanandamayi Devi,[8] known throughout the world as Amma, or Mother, for her selfless love and compassion toward all beings. She pressed Megan to her broad, soft body, patting her back while murmuring, "Mumma, Mumma," and gave her chocolates. As she released Stephen and me, held together, a devotee leaned forward to say that Amma had married us.

AWAKEN *Song*

Awaken, awaken, awaken to the Light in you.
Awaken, awaken, awaken to the Light in you.

See the Light like a waterfall,
Bringing you knowledge, cleansing you;
See the Light of the Father in you,
Guiding and protecting you.

Awaken, awaken, awaken to the Light in you.
Awaken, awaken, awaken to the Light in you.

See the Love of the Mother in you,
Love like a root, giving birth to you.
Light needs Love to awaken in you,
See the Mother creating you.

Awaken, awaken, awaken to the Light in you.
Awaken, awaken, awaken to the Light in you.

PJC 1994

RIVER OF PEACE *Song*

There's a river of light flowing through our hands
from me to you,
And a river of light flowing through our hands
from you to me.
And all we feel is a river of light, joining in harmony,
And all we feel is a river of light, flowing eternally.

There's a river of love flowing through our hearts
from me to you,
And a river of love flowing through our hearts
from you to me.
And all we feel is a river of love, joining in harmony,
And all we feel is a river of love, flowing eternally.

Where the river of light and the river of love become
the river of peace,
The river of peace carries us home in love and unity.
And all we feel is the river of peace, joining in harmony.
And all we feel is the river of peace, flowing eternally.

PJC 1994

CHAPTER 16

Think Love

1995–2001

When you think love you think the moment, when you think love you think you gain. You think love and you are letting go the world you thought was pain. When a brother leaves his body, and we feel the pain inside, it's our lack we're celebrating that without him we would die. We are whole, we are complete, we will suffer no defeat. We have stepped beyond the cross, we're incapable of loss.[1]

Stephen Michael Camp

When Paul Ferrini and Stephen first met, they recognized one another as brothers. Paul was a nationally known, heart-centered spiritual teacher of healing workshops (now given internationally), and among his many books, *Love Without Conditions*[2] became a world-wide best seller. Stephen was building a following for lyrical songs of spiritual truth sung from his heart in a voice of smooth timbre, rich both in depth and high tones. He opened the hearts of his listeners, and, as well, was becoming known as an intuitive healer using vocal sound. Their meeting meant more to Stephen than having a new audience of national participants, as it was his opportunity to work together with a man he admired in a mission he believed in.

When in March 1994 Stephen wanted to move to Florida because it was warmer and was where his clients were, I knew that with Megan in her senior university year I couldn't yet leave. Then a month later he changed his mind and chose to remain up north. But, at that point, considering Stephen's future (and mine), I hired a neighbor to undertake a year-long repair of my home in preparation for its possible future rental. During that year, Stephen frequently sang "Good-bye to New England," a song that he had written for his longing to return to New Mexico. "One of these days I'm gonna say good-bye to New England. One of these days I'm gonna pack my bags and go-oh-oh. Oh and I will say good-bye, and tears will fill my eyes, but I'll take one of her daughters when I go back to New Mexico. Well I miss those mile-high deserts, and I miss those old pueblos, Miss the sun going down most every day-ay-ay, and the promises of rain come drifting 'cross the plain, and, you know, I close my eyes and find I'm standing there in New Mexico."[3] Paul's invitation to Stephen to sing at his Lake Tahoe and Taos workshops answered Stephen's longing.

In June 1995, knowing that it was now time to move to Gainesville, Stephen left, driving a rental truck with our furniture and pulling his Saab, and while we had had times of disagreement, I knew that I would go with him as he had hoped. Meanwhile, I rented my home to a writer friend and her son who moved in while I camped out in my small bedroom in the back extension, crowded in there among all that was still left to take. Completing a grant for creative writing for children and seniors in a neighboring town, I followed in July, driving my Saab on the longest journey I had ever made alone. I arrived to find that Stephen had found an apartment in the same building as the minister of Unity of Gainesville where Stephen would be the principal singer. Villa Ravine was surrounded by tall palms and set back from an avenue. Our six airy rooms were on the second and third (top) floors where off our bedroom was a large, shaded screened porch, with a brook seen through the palms, bubbling along below.

Before we left Massachusetts, a career counselor had told Stephen and me (and I had agreed) that I was "riding on Stephen's coattails." While I used my abilities well and with sincerity, Stephen was rapidly ascending to an awareness of spirit that infused his singing, as he took his listeners on what he called "a journey through light and sound."[4] It is easy to see now how early it was in my training, compared to Stephen's and especially Paul's more indepth awareness of spirituality, but I participated in workshops knowing that I was meant to have those experiences. In Lake Tahoe, I had met a woman who later phoned to say that she had heard this message from Jesus: "I love you just because you exist." Her words stayed with me, and I regretted losing her name, for she had lifted a weight off my heart, teaching me that Jesus's only unit of measure for me was that I had been born.

Camping at Chaco Canyon, the site of the ancestral Pueblo culture, once our one-man tent was set up, I listened to coyotes howling and cooked over a campfire as Stephen strummed his guitar. The next day, farther on in our travels, we stopped on a mountain road for the night where before sleep I lay with my head outside the tent to look at stars. On one occasion Stephen pulled off to the side of a desert road and climbed over wire as I stood watching, until I realized that I'd be left behind if I didn't hurry and follow. He headed a long way across sparse grass then climbed a high hill, with me following, until on top I was balancing across big rocks behind him up to where he sat. Then he showed me petroglyphs (ancient rock drawings) in front of me and pointed across a vastness to where I could see the mountains depicted in the drawings created by some early tribes. Quietly reminiscent, he told me he'd spent many nights there.

At Chapel in Chimayo, while I was standing inside, a statue of Mary had fallen behind me unnoticed until a woman nearby spoke, telling me that was significant for me. There were moments like this...sopapillas (fried pastries) in a small, crowded, sweet smelling restaurant...and I just felt happy being with Stephen in New Mexico.

SANTA FE WEDDING DRESS

What I want is to be married in that white Mexican
sundress hanging in the window of the dress shop
across the brick patio from Casitas.
What I want is to be married before the pomegranate tree
and the ten-foot saguaro
with a hole in its heart where the cactus wren nests
inside the wall that keeps out peccaries and bobcats.
What I want is to be perfect in love,
looking away from angry words
that touch me no more than rain
falling on the other side of the street
in Tucson.
What I'll accept is to be drinking gazpacho,
reading in the shadowed light pierced by hummingbirds,
the *nectar* of your love
two thousand miles away
on my tongue
suddenly
sweet.

PJC 1995

This two-week tour in the Southwest in 1995 gave us time to visit with Marlene, Lorraine, and Carolyn, Stephen's daughters, in California, and then head back to the Southeast, to continue on tour in Alabama, on the eastern shore of Maryland, and in Georgia with brief days at home in between. We returned to Florida just before Christmas, glad to be back in the large city of Gainesville and finally able to begin truly settling into our lovely apartment at Villa Ravine, secluded from the street and restful inside. However, beginning in November, Stephen had, on occasion, been experiencing physical symptoms whose causes he didn't understand but had decided were not serious and possibly had a spiritual intent. At a nod from him, I would take over the workshop when necessary. Unaware that his good-bye was coming for more than New England, we would learn, along with so much else, that by his miscalculation he had produced a miracle.

Three days before Christmas, with Megan visiting on vacation from her university on a return trip to visit her grandmother (Paul's mother) in Sun City, Stephen's headache began and soon escalated to unendurable agony. I was driving. Megan was sitting in back. Startling all three of us, I said—"You're going to have to die." Shocked, he asked what I meant. Hearing my inner voice speak again I added—"You're going to have to die to your fear of death." Two years after Stephen's life ended, the insight came that the first message had been for him, and the second for me. God had veiled our truth.

Not knowing catastrophic insurance had gone into effect two days before (that was the miracle), at home later that night Stephen writhed in torment, refusing to go to a hospital. Desperate, I called Dr. Leonard Smith, a surgeon, who was both a friend and an admirer of Stephen and his music. He left us with no doubts. Going to the hospital, with me in the backseat, holding Stephen up, Megan drove on streets she'd never driven before, saying to me, "I think he's in shock." I concentrated on giving her directions, barely knowing Gainesville's streets myself.

I went into the Emergency Department, and Megan returned to our apartment, where a pot of eggs had boiled over. Smoke had brought the fire department, and they had broken down the door, but our minister helped her lock up. Then she waited for my call.

With his pain heightening, Stephen, unrestrained, physically struggled on the examining table, preventing sedation. I lay across his upper body, weighing down his efforts and two nurses ran in to hold him on either side. When the injection took effect, then it was my waiting. By ten-thirty, the radiologist had diagnosed a mass on the brain. Setting a firm gaze on me, he asked, "Are you hearing me?"

"Yes," I answered, knowing that my life was permanently changed.

Two days later at five-thirty in the morning, I left the hospital where I had slept on the visitor's room floor to get Stephen's Harris Tweed jacket and guitar. We then left, walking out the door with a doctor following, saying we couldn't. By ten o'clock, Megan and I were seated in the front row of Unity of Gainesville for the Christmas service, while, as the principal singer, Stephen sat up front, facing us. The congregation had been told moments before we entered, the last ones to come in. When he sang "O Little Town of Bethlehem," I saw stars fill his head. Thinking he would be fine, I instead would learn that the cancer cells were star-shaped.

On January 3, the admissions officer of the Malcolm Randall VA Medical Center quietly told us the seriousness of Stephen's condition. The diagnosis: a glialblastoma, Grade IV, the most aggressive form of brain cancer, and the treatment was immediate surgery and radiation. Stephen, turning to where I sat behind him, asked, "Will you marry me?" We were engaged, and I looked down at the gold and turquoise ring he'd had made in

Lake Tahoe. Reassuring him, I excused myself and called Beth, who asked the right question. I returned to answer Yes. Given two hours to get a license and find our minister to sign the paper, we met him in the parking lot of Villa Ravine, and we were married.

In March 1996, we would reverse our roles. Where Stephen had been the guest minister and singer on tour and I his workshop helper, on this Sunday morning in a Unity Church, I was the minister while he sang. My talk was "A Love beyond Time," and in it I shared the words he had spoken to me that momentous night at *A Course in Miracles* when he had told me that he had always loved me but was waiting for me to figure that out. I had come to see his words of love for me as God's words of love for each of us. God *was* always there and only waiting for us to figure that out.

That was the month we bogged down, reshaping a life from remnants no longer useful. Stephen's daughters had come to see him between the time of his surgery and June when he went to San Diego, where they lived, as we had found a clinic for alternative treatment there so they could visit with him. I later silently thanked them for taking him where he asked, to a Mexican restaurant, so he could eat his last enchiladas and black beans. At home, at the alternative clinic, and later at the hospital, he was on a doctor-recommended diet.

Meanwhile, we received five thousand dollars from both his mother and my father. I sold his tapes nationally (raising thirty thousand dollars) and recorded a daily message about his condition for people around the country who loved him and were calling. Their messages inspired, comforted, strengthened, and educated me as of the hundreds, only two spoke of sadness and loss, while all others affirmed the presence of a loving God. The wife of a survivor of a similar (but earlier grade) brain cancer offered me copies of her easy, low-calorie-dish cookbook, along with their story of courage. Grateful, I took the colorful, red and white tablecloth-covered books to local bookstores, where kind owners put them on their shelves.

In April, when Paul Ferrini called to gently remind me that everyone is important and others were in conditions similar to Stephen's and mine, his words reached my heart where I hadn't been aware. I felt grateful for his caring as I was trying to do all that I could, with every step I took being a first-time experience. He was like an older brother helping. With Paul's encouraging me to take time for myself, three months after Stephen's surgery, his mother came from Tennessee, and I went to New York City to speak at Interfaith Fellowship in Cami Hall. Invited by its co-founders, Dr. Jon Mundy[5] and Rev. Dr. Diane Berke,[6] I took a week to give myself the rest I needed. In the closing moments of the service, hundreds of small, white candles suddenly were lit, illuminating the depth of rows in the large, darkened hall in one of the most quieting and beautiful ceremonies I have ever attended.

On the day Stephen was ready to leave California, we were to meet in Houston, where he'd been accepted for a protocol at the Burzynski Clinic that had required congressional approval. In Florida and driving alone to Orlando International Airport, I uncharacteristically missed the turn and instead found that I was on I-75 heading instead to Tampa. Realizing the seriousness of my mistake, I sped up to eighty, invisibly passing state troopers parked and talking, but upon seeing a third shortly after, bounced my car to a stop, and barely waiting for his question, replied that I knew I was doing eighty-two—Could he help me? With his directions and assurance that I'd make it, I continued at eighty, eyeing the gas gauge on empty as I reached the airport approach roads. Parking in front of the terminal, I ran to the counter only to learn I'd missed the flight by misreading my ticket. An airport manager took my car keys as I followed an agent to another airline that took me on board. In Houston I reached the right gate in time to watch Stephen, with little stability, weave forward, searching for me where I stood, my hands on a wheelchair.

At the home of a Unity of Houston couple who'd volunteered their help, I met Dr. Smith who'd arrived from Florida. Looking at me, he quietly yet clearly said, "Moribund." Searching my vocabulary, I sensed the meaning.

For fourteen weeks, we commuted to Houston in four-seat private planes, flown by volunteer pilots, one of whom was Patrick Lyndon Nugent, whose flying by local landmarks became my moments of humor. I couldn't see the buildings, rivers, and highways that they could, but enjoyed being close to the ground. Behind me, Stephen smiled under his baseball cap, as lower air pressure abated his pain.

By October 1996, almost a year after the first symptoms had appeared without our comprehending their seriousness, the Burzynski Clinic and the Malcolm Randall VA Medical Center were working cooperatively. I lived at the hospital, trained in Houston to give intravenous treatments, unaware that when Stephen was moved to a private room, the medical staff had formed a conclusion.

Each time he re-entered the hospital, I made it home. Family photos and scenes of New Mexico were within his view. His thick, red bathrobe lay across the white sheet. Once I carried steaming rice cooked in the nurses' kitchen past where they were eating cold pizza. The blender whirred at four-hour intervals with a nutritional shake he'd slurp, whispering, "Delicious." With little strength, one time he managed to reach out, his arm brushing across my breast, amazing me with his remaining masculinity as I responded to our unexpected intimacy.

When he needed tests, I pushed the gurney through long, echoing corridors, learning routes and acting as if I were a nurse. I'd bend over, moving, and kiss him quickly, upside down, causing stares. Or speed through a vacant area, gaining a daring moment in the smallest world we'd known.

Prior to each hospital test he needed, I stood over him on our king-size waterbed, pulling him up by his arms. From the first, his refrain was, "You are so strong. You are so beautiful." He may have wondered if I'd give up on him—or, in despair at times, wished I would; but I kept a mental picture of his daughters' hopes, along with my own, knowing I would do all that I could for him.

Once his legs had dropped over the bed, it was an effort for the two of us to get him to the stairs, and then easier. He sat and I pulled him, bumping, down. The day he fell getting into the car backed close to the apartment, I'd hauled him up like a 160-pound rag doll onto the front seat. That may have been when he told me he couldn't see as well, and I had experienced an epiphany, saying under my breath, "Thank you, God." By then, I'd become worn to the truth that things happened beyond my control. I could accept or complain. I chose to begin affirming everything, hoping this was what I was to know about God.

HERE

Here in the VA examining room
I cradle Stephen's head
above the rigid arms of his wheelchair.
A clear plastic line
hangs from a metal pole,
dripping life back to where
it has tried to ebb:
another rescue.
His head is a pressurized drink
he moves left and right,
wanting to open the cap.

Beside me Jane Kenyon's poetry
calms me. I read of February
in New Hampshire,
a poem far from muggy Florida
where my car's parked
by the emergency entrance—
indefinitely.

PJC 1996

The day Stephen softly, slowly, carefully spelled "s t e p h e n," then "l i g h t," I knew he was seeing in another dimension. He told me there were Indians in the closet, but I said no, later regretting my answer as I had seen American Indians in visions. In the only mode I knew of keeping him alive, telling him yes in a comforting voice would have been beyond my current state at that point. Admitting the guides were there would confirm he was leaving, and I wasn't ready.

On October 6, I was returning to his room after a visit with the chief medical officer when my inner voice spoke a firm, serious message I did not expect nor would avoid. I heard "He really wants to leave. There's a slim chance he will stay, but he has to have ultimate peace." Knowing the sound of truth, I answered, "I passionately adore you and am thinking of your daughters, but if you need to leave, I give you my permission." That afternoon I returned with a letter from his youngest daughter Carolyn that had just arrived. Seeing the letter firmly held now between his fingers, I recognized a blessing from Jesus, brought to a man who at times I had seen hold his head in his hands and say, "Jesus," certain that He was always there.

By early evening, his pulse stopped. I asked for resuscitation, and stood unmovable in the doorway. Repeating the Twenty-third Psalm, watching the procedure that followed, it was the only decision I would later regret. Yet, in the moment, surprised and comforted, I saw and felt the presence of huge angels, strong, waiting on magnificent white horses. I heard "Warrior Angels" and have not heard that name nor seen them since.

For two hours I talked to him of the love for him by his family, his friends, and workshop followers, intermingled with moments of singing his songs and stroking his body. His breath rose and fell through an oxygen mask, until a little intake and then stillness told me his soul had left. Helping with the body bag, I put photos of Jesus and Marlene, Lorraine, and Carolyn, and my pink tee shirt on his bare chest for the journey. As a nurse pushed the gurney toward the door, I told her I would push him alone, and turned it around so he traveled headfirst. "I Am A Shepherd's Child,"[7] his favorite song, played from a tape recorder on his chest, echoing in the late evening emptiness. At the freezer, I spoke my parting words, "It's not as warm as New Mexico, but where you are, you're fine." Then I called friends to come empty the room. They told me a hurricane had passed through.

By choice, I went home alone. Getting out of the car, I stood and looked at the full moon. In that pause, I heard the first line of a new song. I sang it, knowing the melody as well. "Oh full moon," then the second, "Pouring down love," and a third, "I love you Stephen," with a longer pause. There was nothing new. Then the gentle shock came. "*Love* is loving." I was not to make it inside the apartment without the lesson that love is more than loving one person. Love is the act of loving. When I unwrapped a package that had arrived, with a book inside, I opened it randomly and read that a storm comes when a great soul passes.

Having no experience of what to do at a cremation, I sat on one side of the crematorium reading from *A Course in Miracles* then moved to the other side, where I quietly beat my Taos drum. An aura of green light hovered along the roofline. When the box was put in my hands, my heart and thoughts startled from the warmth, as I hadn't expected a box of ashes to feel good. Helping myself make the parting memorable, I headed for an Indian restaurant that would be Stephen's choice, placed a napkin over the box in my lap and ordered, saying, "My husband may be coming late; please set a place." That night, lying back on the enormous bed, I removed the bag of ashes, placed them on my chest, and promptly fell asleep. "He is still comforting me with his warmth," were my last sleepy words.

I looked at my remaining options and decided on a different experience from a traditional memorial service, unaware that my desire was a quiescent seed for the future. There would be two evenings of celebration: a wedding ceremony on the Friday night after Thanksgiving, as we hadn't had a ceremony (allowed only those two hours to leave the hospital to have the marriage license signed), and a Remembrance on Saturday evening, giving his daughters six weeks to help them face this ending after ten months of an emotional drain, and giving me time to feel the hardest grief and begin transforming it to gratitude, and to rest.

Opening the Remembrance, I told those gathered that they would laugh as well as cry. Rev. Bill Cameron, the senior minister of Unity on the Bay in Miami had come, and beautifully did all I asked to support my role as minister with him. From our friendship, I knew his wisdom, compassion, and joy would be the underpinning I wanted and needed to make the memory of this day I mentally pictured come alive for me as well as for all who had gathered with us.

Our sadness was palpable. But I intended laughter too. I'd found two cassettes in Stephen's collection of a thousand that when listened to out of curiosity had reduced me to near-unstoppable laughter until laughing-tears soaked my cheeks. This was how I wanted him remembered as well. And so the first I played was his imitation of Julia Child, the indomitable French Chef. He spoke with a French accent, then a German, then a British one, telling how to make nonsense recipes he'd invented. It worked! Laughter lifted up the church.

The second cassette required my first and last karaoke performance. Stephen was playing "Sweet Surrender," "Oh sweet surrender, I surrender to the will of the Lord,"[8] a good message for the celebration. But he wasn't playing the way he did in church. He was strumming strongly, swiftly, sensually, making the guitar vibrate and letting out his voice as if he were onstage at an outdoor concert. I had been dancing rather wildly around the living room when he'd stopped and told me, "Go check the carrots," then continued. Braving the potential embarrassment of five daughters, I took his guitar out of its case from where I'd put that on the platform, started the tape, and imitated him singing and playing. At his cooking direction, I let the guitar drop on the strap, rushed to a brown supermarket bag, pulled out a pot and carrots, put the carrots in the pot, then rushed back to finish his song. The laughter washed over my relief. It was these things few people knew about him that I wanted them to know now.

His first grandson, six months old, was passed from arms to arms, his babyhood softening grief. My sister took him last and stood in the back, gently swaying him until the end of the ceremony. When the guests had left and the church was being returned to order, an overhead track of lights began blinking on and off. Someone went to flip the switch, but for thirty minutes they wouldn't turn off. Megan wanted to know, "Is that him?" and I smiled—"Yes."

Then Paul Ferrini entered our lives once more, by writing a tenderly worded, wisely truthful eulogy of Stephen's full journey. In words like the touch of a thrown stone as it skims over the water, he fully captured Stephen's essence in "The Certainty of the Leaves," to be found in this excerpt from *Crossing the Water*: "And as you take leave of us, know it is not your songs we love best, but the man who sang them, the man who softened and let himself be known, the man who opened and let himself be loved."[9]

A week after Stephen's passing, a woman I didn't know well, but trusted, had told me that her teacher had said I would be fine, and would marry again. I had been a widow one week. But while it seemed too soon for those words, I accepted that she wanted to soothe me from her heart. I had begun following my own recovery program. Sudden outbursts of sobbing that caused me to drop to my knees for a loss of strength gradually lessened with teachings I knew were truth. "God, I know this is best for Stephen, and best for me. I'm just not used to it yet." Each time, I would feel pale blue light descend as a cape around me and a deep inner peace quiet me. I could communicate with Stephen and often saw an identical version of him pass me biking or driving, experiences that I mentally and emotionally recorded but didn't understand.

After the November remembrances, my plans were to leave Florida for two months and then return to face decisions about my life, my being alone and without work.

During the first week of December, I drove out of the South weighing one hundred and one pounds, my long hair layered to three inches. I had carefully decided to go first to Connecticut and then to Wisconsin to be with Beth and Megan for Christmas and New Year's. Stirred by excitement—it would be good to do something I ordinarily wouldn't—I closed my eyes to the cost and signed up for three events: a week-long writing intensive in Amherst, a conference at a Unity Church in Atlanta, and back home, a reading by a man unknown to me except through one of the doctors who as Stephen's friend had helped us. Six times I listened to this doctor insist that I come to the workshops he was sponsoring, until finally, realizing this was a way I could thank him, I agreed to go to one reading *only,* unaware that in that reading, I would learn of my new and strong direction.

As Beth and Megan let me find my own way through their family holiday activities, I was comforted being near them and my feelings of aloneness softened. Remembering how two years ago, I'd been in warm, flowering San Diego on New Year's morning, signing the words to "I Find Peace" as several hundred listened to Stephen sing, I watched snow fall out beyond the aroma of crusty-brown turkey. While vodka cocktails were lifted in noisy conversation, I sat in the warmth from the home's quiet furnace, seeking balance in gratitude.

Through January, I moved toward inner and outer acceptance. I wrote in Pat's workshop, feeling safe in the familiar room of floor-to-ceiling books, slipping easily back into the writing process. Words of pain that had at first poured onto paper metamorphosed into positive writing by the final ceremony.

Days later in Atlanta, seated among 2,000 women and a few men, I was mentally jolted by medical intuitive and world renowned speaker Caroline Myss'[10] information and, in the wit of her truth, felt my own tension release as my muscles relaxed in bursts of laughter.

Then back home at the end of January, in the reading I had signed up for, I met the man who would begin to guide me through a future I could not have imagined.

One evening after dark, as I was gazing out the dining room's full wall of glass at a small, spotlight-lit bough of a narrow evergreen tree, I saw Stephen's face, formed by the tree's shadows. It would have been baseball size except that it was only the left half, for the right wasn't visible. It was as if the right side was behind the trunk.

First startled by the exact image, then fascinated, and next apprehensive, I backed away, keeping my eyes on his face, then went closer, then moved away...six times...until going upstairs, I looked down from my office window's full wall of glass and could still see him.

For six nights I watched, each night again checking from upstairs (as if something might change). I continued to feel both comforted and slightly unnerved, as I had no understanding of "how?"

Later I wondered why I hadn't taken a photo, but I'd had the earlier experiences (and would have more) of seeing duplicates and each time only watched.

Over the following five years, when brief moments of intense memory returned, I'd remember "the seventh wave" I'd learned about as a child. It was bigger, and if my back was to the waves, it could surprise me forward and take me under.

PERHAPS

Perhaps I would have kissed him
more, held his head in my hands
and cupped my courage
for him to hear directly.
Instead I combed his hair,
his eyebrows...trimming the wild
thoughts back to conform
to the shape I found attractive.

PJC   1997

Tears came and tears left, until, at the five-year mark, I presented Stephen's message and his music at the Seraphim Center a final time. The seats were filled, and I saw tears. But I spoke with
clarity and sincerity in assurance that the two gifts he'd given me
were his coming into my life, and his leaving. That had happened.
That was God. I knew *all* came from God and was good. In my
surrender, I'd found truth.

Stephen had found his peace...and left us with a song reminding
us that as he had we could too. "I find peace is here in this world
today. I feel love is here in our hearts to stay. I see the light, guiding
our way. You and I are only here to say...I find peace."[11] All he had
wanted was to sing his songs to God, and he had done that.

Writing about Stephen for this book, I contacted Paul Ferrini for the first time in eighteen years and from our short emails,
with love, ordered *Love Without Conditions*. In the introduction
I found his channeled words in the simple and clear writing that
I prefer that entered my heart, "You are responsible for any teaching you accept as truth. No one else has that responsibility. In
the end, experience is the best teacher. Experience shows us what
works and what does not, what helps and what hurts."[12] For twenty years I have been conscious that to learn I have had to experience. When the next spiritual teacher I met in my reading had
brought Meher Baba into my life, in time I would read in *God
Speaks* the same truth, "God cannot be explained, He cannot be
argued about, He cannot be theorized, nor can He be discussed
and understood. God can only be lived.... Reality can never be
understood; it is to be realized by conscious experience."[13]

In his channeling of Jesus, Paul Ferrini became a living bridge
from my past to my present, perhaps sent as a third gift from the
spirit of a man with whom I traveled in the world, entering spiritual truth more deeply in our saga of six years.

WILLING

Each time I brush my teeth, I see my husband—
his mouth foaming with toothpaste, his eyes
dark, focused. It's three months since he died.
A guru called a memory a hungry ghost.
Well, I want my ghosts to be well fed.
I want to see those brushings as a measurement
of my husband loving life and me... his
willingness for the alternative... a gift of love.

PJC 1997

HEALING *Song*

Written at Pat's AWA workshop three months after
Stephen took his last breath, about a time long before
when I had directed my anger at my first husband, who
had loved me and was the father of our daughters, as if
Stephen's import on my life now caused self-discovery
and healing to be born as song.

When you're in pain,
it's so easy to blame
the one you love more
than any other.
It's hard to explain,
but there's nothing to gain
by sending your hurt to another.
Try to resist making a fist
or listing a history of wrongs.
The only way to win
is to go within;
it's you that you see
reflected in the other.

PJC 1997

BELIEVING

CHAPTER 17

April to May

1997

It is an unalterable and universally
recognized fact since time immemorial
that God knows everything. God does
everything, and that nothing happens
but by the Will of God... He is the
Creator, the Producer, the Actor and
the Audience in His own Divine Plan[1]

Meher Baba

On January 31, 1997, I met David Cousins, a spiritual master, mystic, healer, and author of *A Handbook for Light Workers*,[2] who unbeknown to me would begin the next phase of my spiritual journey. That day in Gainesville, he gave me the first of numerous readings that lasted for forty-five minutes as he spoke in both a straightforward manner and through metaphor. At our first meeting, feeling strengthened by having driven 3,000 miles alone for the first time, and feeling my energy reviving, I listened in amazement and with concentration as he interrupted himself with little smiles, quietly describing me as having no self-love or self-esteem—a spiritual child who would grow into a spiritual adult taking 100 percent responsibility for her life. My hubby, he said, was sending down lots of love, but he had been a stepping-stone, and I hadn't yet done what I'd come to the planet to do. I needed to let go of the husband and get on with life, or I would lose mine. I heard there was a next man who had me in his little black book, who was a very fast lightworker,[3] like the driver of a London double-decker bus who didn't stop for red lights. He then told me of Meher Baba, who I didn't know of, and heard that he was standing behind me, cranking up my heart that was all run-down. David added that while I looked as if I were ready to join my husband, that wasn't going to happen, because I was actually taking on energy nicely. As a feeling of safety kept growing, I felt my tense posture gradually relax.

It had been a year and a half since Stephen and I had arrived in Florida. Not fully unpacked from that move, I now had begun clearing away my husband's things, which included even his kindergarten reports. The effort would take nine months. Having signed up for only the one reading with David, afterwards I found myself susceptible to the light in this man's eyes, his gentle demeanor, his unusual metaphors of what my life would be, his small chuckles diverting me from the seriousness of his words—"It's like this: you are in a hot air balloon a mile above the earth, where, at three miles up, you'll be able to see more, but not as much as I can from six miles up"—and I took the last open place in the following day's workshop. There, in an exercise listening to outer space-sounding music, I matched my hands to his and, as we raised them, looking into each other's eyes, I heard myself say, "I have been waiting so long for you to come" ... and thought, "Unusual." That afternoon, he told us to begin repeating four names that he gave us for sixteen minutes each day until only one name remained: Om Sai Ram, Meerama, Lord Jesus, and Meher Baba. Every morning and afternoon, I walked a short distance to Alfred A. Ring Park, where my feet liked the feel of the wooden boardwalk making its way through palmetto and pine along the Hogtown Creek, until by the first week of February, Meher Baba was the only name I repeated. "You might want to go to India in the fall," David told me, but said that I didn't have to and then pausing, added, "Although you are a journey person."

David returned to Florida in April, and at my reading he said that the sun would open its front door and its back door, and that was my clue. I learned that a big Red Indian with bearskins to cloak me would take me up *his* mountain, passing by many people in a line, along with extraterrestrials. Meher Baba was on top, playing a lamenting tune—as he was calling me but I wasn't answering.

The next day I called friends, but no one had heard of Meher Baba. The following day, a dim memory of Myrtle Beach surfaced, and, dialing information, I asked for Meher Baba's phone number. There was no such listing. Then I asked for any number with either of those names and was given the phone number of a Meher Center in South Carolina. Feeling relief, with my call I learned that this center was Meher Baba's official home in America, and I arranged to visit in August.

Two hours later, my phone rang with a call from a man I didn't know, whose name I had forgotten by the middle of our conversation (Jesse Massa). I told him something I usually wouldn't, but what I remember is that when I mentioned Meher Baba, he hollered so loudly I pulled the phone away. With the phone back to my ear, I heard that he would meet me and give me photos of Meher Baba when he returned from a trip. I had found a connection to Meher Baba. In a second call I learned that his name was Jesse, but not until a year later did I realize that he'd given me my first official Meher Baba greeting of "Jai Baba."

David's metaphors materialized in a natural way, integrated into my daily living. I found them interesting but except for once in three years, I didn't ask for explanations. So when David said in a reading, "The bird will come, the bat will come, the fox will come, the wolf will come, and the bird will come again," I thought, "That's interesting," until the night the bird appeared—then it became *very* interesting for what I learned. As I was walking under a trellis covered in a profusion of flowering vines, going to the apartment pool, I heard a bird chirping so loudly that I stopped to look up and identify it. It was a cardinal. Later, looking up the meaning of cardinal in Jamie Sams' and David Carson's *Medicine Cards*,[4] a book of Native American animal messages, I found that cardinal meant renewed self-esteem, and I smiled with pleasure.

A few days later, having supper by the pool, a bat flew over then returned, continuing its pattern until a young couple appeared, diverting my attention. They were soaked with sweat, and I asked if they'd been jogging, but learned that they'd been to a gym. As I'd been told by David, "As you put on weight..." without an end to the sentence, I concluded that I must need to go to a gym, but didn't know of one. Looking up both the bat and the couple's gym, I learned that bat meant rebirth and the gym was one with black rubber floor mats and no high-mounted TVs, where mostly men lifted weights. I went in May. On my first visit, I waited for the woman ahead of me to sign in. About to write my name, I noticed hers with amusement. It was Barbara Jesse—my first name followed by the first name of the man who'd called with a "Jai Baba."

Each week I began at the treadmill, and as I picked up speed, I saw a vision of an older man with thinning dark hair pulled back, wearing a long, white dress aslant on one shoulder, dancing. I didn't know who he was, but I liked watching.

By May, the fox, the wolf, and the final bird, a robin, had appeared during a network chiropractic treatment. I made a list of the fifteen past lives I had seen in that session for this favorite doctor, and he told me that while he didn't see visions, he'd never seen anyone's spine change as much as mine had that day. Face down on his table, I had seen my life as a fox and watched as I, the fox, was hunted by hounds, attacked by a bear, and after this, appeared as a vixen with kits. I could both see the cubs and feel them snuggled against my own shoulder. Fox means camouflage, and later I would learn to keep my occult experiences more hidden. As a wolf traveling alone, I had died and watched my soul visibly lift up, teaching me that the wolf had a soul. An Indian on horseback crossed the river flowing behind me to the bank where I lay. Wolf means family and teacher, and I had been a teacher. I identified the final bird of the metaphor when, still face down on the chiropractor's table, a robin had appeared, singing to me. Robin means new growth in all areas.

The last week of May, I'd spoken again to Jesse. He had photos of Meher Baba to give me and on this day I was in his town. On my call, he invited me to the farm. Going in the front door I momentarily sat on the sofa, until he began sharing his feelings about an experience related to his first call. Seeing an orchard through the open sliding glass door and needing to feel more comfortable, I asked if we could first take a walk through the field. When we stopped at the back fence, watching the neighbor's horses, I felt like putting my arm around his waist, but held it straight down, confused by my inappropriate thought. It would be fall before I understood. Back on the sofa and looking at my first photos of Meher Baba, I recognized the image as my dancer-vision from the gym.

As I was ready to leave after our visit, Jesse invited me to a fair, to swim at the springs, or have coffee, but I had travel plans for June and couldn't accept. He was leaving for a six-months' stay at Meherabad, also in June, and when he asked if I would write I agreed.

CHAPTER 18

June to July

1997

Self-awareness—recognizing a feeling as
it happens—is the keystone of emotional
intelligence.[1]

Daniel Goleman

My June travel plans to visit my family also included honoring a commitment Stephen had made to be the principal speaker at a conference of Coptic priests near Barbara Hero's home in Maine. It was important to me to present Stephen's work, and I felt gratified that Barbara welcomed my taking his place. Remembering two years ago my darshan with Amma, who I have written about in "Love, Serve, Forgive," and her warm and loving hugs, I looked at her schedule and learned that she would be giving a weekend-long darshan near where my dad then lived. I hoped that I could arrange to go as part of my new life.

My roommate from the Ira Progoff *Intensive Journal* workshop and I had kept in touch through my move to Florida years later, and now stopping at her home in New Jersey on my drive to New England, she gave me a reading. As she was finishing, I lifted my gaze from her face to behind her where I saw a hawk flying directly at the back kitchen door. Telling her, we both immediately stood, knowing this was significant, and stepped out into her front yard. Above us were more than twenty hawks circling over us as we watched, unmoving. The last notes of information in her reading had been about Egypt and Stephen, and we understood this as being connected to the hawks, defined in animal symbolism as messengers. We stood until the sky was empty.

Now temporarily staying at my home in Longmeadow, on the morning I was to make the two-and-a-half-hour drive from Western Massachusetts to Smithfield for Amma's appearance, I awoke at five a.m. with my throat too sore to swallow. Lying in bed knowing that I had to arrive by ten o'clock and determined that I would, I gargled with warm salt water, packed a sari from a friend who had lived in the Far East, and left.

When I arrived at the registration desk, my papers showed that I had left the line for a spiritual name blank. For several months, I had been mulling over names, wanting one that would have a softer sound than Barbara. Prema had kept coming to me, but I hadn't felt worthy of its meaning of "divine love." This morning, waiting to sign in, a change occurred—I wanted to be Prema. When the woman behind the table sternly questioned me, pointing out that I hadn't given a spiritual name on my application, and therefore had to use Barbara, I firmly repeated that Prema was the name I wanted. Due to my determination that I was not going to change my position—or perhaps to her recognition of my sincerity—she finally relented. With relief, I left for the cafeteria and kitchen duty. As I walked, I noticed that my throat felt fine and my wrist with my name band was encircled with pink light. I'd found my courage.

Having slowly moved through a long line, I was at last facing Amma. She pressed me tightly to her full, soft bosom, until as she stopped patting and began loosening her arms, instead of continuing to straighten, I paused and leaning toward her again, whispered, "I am God," meaning God is in *everyone*. Quickly she pulled me back for more pats and more chocolate.

When my roommate told me that Amma chose spiritual names, I considered asking, but my new dilemma was that she might give me one other than Prema. When I shared my concern, I learned that there was a line for people with questions where I could ask Amma to bless my name. I handed my paper to the young woman interpreting for Amma, who continued to give hugs to each person in the advancing line as she listened to her interpreter reading the papers. When it was my turn, I concentrated on Amma. Then as her interpreter turned to me, I heard that my name Prema had been blessed.

Soon I would remember Stephen's and my flight from India in 1994, when in the final two hours approaching New York, he had rapidly written three songs, one of which was "The Embodiment of Love (Prema Swarupa)." That seed waiting for the right moment of inspiration for my name had now germinated.

Hours later, as a thousand people were leaving the closing circle, I saw a woman with a white cane who I had noticed before. Approaching her, I said, "I'm Prema," and hugging her had immediately felt her hug back, also hearing that Amma had just named *her* Prema. At the time I found our sharing a name amazing—that out of all of the people there, I had been drawn only to her? But I think it was by grace. She could not see how many were surrounding us, and I wanted her to feel the warmth of my hug—of a woman wanting to connect with her.

Headed then to visit my dad, who lived a short drive south of Smithfield, and at last standing at the door of his Greenwich Bay apartment, I knocked and waited. As he opened the door, from his first view of me he looked mildly flustered—it was the tangerine sari I was still wearing. I was being drawn closer to eastern spirituality, and he didn't know what to make of it.

A postcard from Jesse was waiting (I had given him my dad's address). I felt pleased but didn't reply because I was preparing to leave for my speaking engagement in Maine. As I was getting ready, my dad asked to accompany me. Surprised, I was definitely pleased. Upon our arrival at the location given for the conference, when we first entered the room I had momentarily turned aside, and as I turned back I discovered my 6 foot 4¾ inch father had compacted his height into a small (for him) "egg" shape at the feet of one of the men greeters, and at that moment I didn't recognize why.

For my talk, I had gone through Stephen's materials, relieved and grateful to find a cassette recording of a song that he had written specifically for his presentation. When I had played it I heard that he referred to the Nile River. While I could not give the information as he would have, I was familiar with his work and could speak of it in my words, plus I had the unexpected gift of his recording bringing Stephen and his knowledge as close to those listening as I could.

Later, when I questioned my father about what had appeared

to me to be a bow before the greeter that morning, he told me with naturalness and no affectation that he had simply wanted to honor the man. While I considered that he might have been honoring me as a presenter, and showing appreciation for coming by participating, what I came to understand is that the souls of these two men had had a past life together in Egypt. There had been recognition, and this was a reunion. In the future, a spiritual teacher would refer to me as a favorite daughter of my father's in an Egyptian lifetime, which later happily added meaning to my dad's being with me.

Before we left the conference, the singer, whose name was my birth name, Barbara, had asked if we could exchange readings. In hers, she told me that my husband was sending down "salmon-pink" light—a color I hadn't heard of, but it sounded pretty—and also that I was going to "write and write and write"—interesting to me as I had no plans for writing.

Returning now to the day in June when I had left my Villa Ravine apartment in Florida, as I was traveling north on I-95, an eighteen-wheeler passed me, and glancing up, then staring, I saw Jesse's name in big letters on the side. How could a big carrier have *his* name? Trucks had company names; Jesse was not a common name. But through June and July, not only on the East Coast but also the West Coast where I visited Stephen's daughters, I continued seeing Jesse's name. Finally I started a list beginning with the eighteen-wheeler. A Jesse had let me into a private apartment building in Back Bay Boston—I knew by his name badge. Going to a Northampton, Massachusetts restaurant for lunch, I had seen a bureau against a wall with a photo and a sweet memorial for a Jesse, who was the baby son of the owners. A Jesse was the overheard topic of my seatmates' conversation on a flight to California, and in San Diego it was a Jesse who rented a car to me. I read of a Jesse in a newspaper, in a book I bought, and of two, father and son, on a poster entering a supermarket. By late July or early August when I had sixty entries I stopped. Holding a one-sided conversation with Meher Baba, I told Him that I didn't know who *He* was, but I understood that this man Jesse was certainly important.

At some point during June or July I had figured out that Jesse was the very fast lightworker David had told me about and Jesse's farm the place where the sun had opened its front door and its back door—only much later realizing the sun was a metaphor for Meher Baba. Years later, reading of Meher Baba, I found words to remind me of that summer: "Your Baba is always with you; even if you wanted to leave Him you cannot do so."² From my viewpoint, He hadn't been "my Baba" that summer, but from His viewpoint, He was.

CHAPTER 19

August

1997

Meher Spiritual Center is a spiritual retreat for
rest, meditation, and renewal of the spiritual life,
for those who love and follow Meher Baba, and
for those who know of him and want to know
more.... Five hundred acres of dense forest ad-
jacent to the Atlantic Ocean and two fresh-water
lakes provide a peaceful natural setting.[1]

Meher Spiritual Center

In February, David had told me that I might want to go to India in the fall, but that I didn't have to. I had listened but felt no urge to make a decision. In April, pressed by his words that Meher Baba was calling me and I wasn't answering, I had located the Meher Spiritual Center in North Myrtle Beach, South Carolina and had made my August reservation for three days, during my return trip to Florida.

Finding the nearly hidden entrance along the woodsy stretch of North Kings Highway, I registered for my first visit then slowly drove from the Gate Lodge through tall trees on a winding, sand road enveloped by greenery and (except for the engine's hum) a serene quietude. Ending up at a parking lot near my cabin, I faced my new experience—excited and apprehensive. The view opened from the hilltop to a lake that, up close, revealed turtles' heads, big, silver-hued fish erupting in splashes, and alligator backs. Beyond were the dunes of the Atlantic Ocean.

On the morning that I went to Meher Baba's house, glancing around, I had looked into a round, glass display case, and with a sudden intake of breath upon seeing Meher Baba's "salmon-pink" coat, I understood then that it had not been my husband who had sent the light in June but Meher Baba, disguising His entrance into my life.

It was during this visit that I saw my first video of Him, and watching, unexpected tears fell, ignored as they dripped onto my lap. He was wearing a coat of that same pink color and long, sheer white fabric that flowed around his legs from the fast pace He set as He strode around a flower garden, repeatedly turning, attentive to the camera. When He stood close, facing into it, I believed He was gazing directly at me. Overwhelmed, I realized that I'd seen pictures of Jesus, but was now watching God, walking.

On the third day, when I was to leave, my car needed repair, so I drove to a recommended garage on King's Highway and discovered that I could walk back to the center along the beach. By the ninth day, again ready to leave, my car again needed repair, and this time I knew that it had nothing to do with my car, but with Meher Baba.

On one of my previous days, driving on an errand, I had heard a new, stronger, more forceful inner voice give a brief command. I'd promptly asked, "Who are you?" and heard, "the Ancient One." As in delayed recognition of someone newly met, I realized this was what Meher Baba called Himself.

Now on my tenth and final day, as I was having lunch with my new roommate who had arrived at the Hill Cabin the night before, I eventually said to her, "I didn't meet Baba, I didn't meet Mehera, and I didn't meet Mani. Who's left to meet?" (Mehera was His Beloved and Mani was His sister.) Her immediate reply was, "Why, you'll come to my home and meet Bhau!" My roommate lived in Chicago. I was driving from Massachusetts to Florida and due to return to Virginia in two weeks. For three seconds I considered her invitation—then answered that I would. I had never been to Chicago nor had I driven through the Appalachian Mountains. For that matter, the drive here had been only my second time driving the East Coast fully, and only years later would I realize that Meher Baba had given me the courage and strength to do this. Arriving at this large meeting of Meher Baba lovers who were there in Chicago to see Bhau Kalchuri, the beloved Chairman of the Meher Baba Trust who was then touring America, Bhau Kalchuri welcomed me with an immediate hug.

Briefly returning from Chicago to the Center, I ended my August visit at Meher Center in the small, square, dark green Lagoon Cabin where Meher Baba had held interviews in the 1950s, and where I now sat quietly. It was not only near my present housing at Cabin on the Hill but also near the curved wooden steps down to the footbridge over the inlet where I'd often paused to look at the water lilies. Kneeling in the cabin on this near-final day, as I would be leaving in the morning, I had faced His large photo and then, by a quarter-turn, His chair. A shawl of lamplight barely lit the demure fabric and dulled-wood gleam of earlier-style furniture but was brighter on the cut flowers gracing the table. David had told me that I would have "an esoteric cup of tea" with Baba, and it was then that I saw a cup and saucer, thin as a veil, briefly float before me.

Accepting tea from Meher Baba changed my life's journey, and I considered that for my second Christmas without Stephen, journeying to Meherabad, might be the answer that would light a flame in me and strengthen my self-confidence.

I left for Richmond, Virginia as a guest minister at two Unity Churches, where one woman greeted me with a hug and a reassuring comment. She said thoughtfully that I was truly peaceful inside. My talk was "A Love Beyond Time" taken from that life-altering night at *A Course in Miracles* when Stephen had told me that he had always loved me and had been waiting for me to figure it out. I had come to realize that he was defining God's love. God *is* always there, waiting for us to figure that out.

Soon after returning to my apartment, in late August, I left for Miami where I was scheduled to give psychic readings and stay with friends of Stephen's and mine who had invited me to their houseboat. Late one night, as I listened to water lapping the sides with my notepad on my lap, I began writing automatically. My pen moved across the paper without any thought: "No matter what he says or does, you are only to treat him with kindness. It has taken him many lifetimes to prepare for this one with you." I knew immediately who the words were about—they could only be about Jesse. But the words were for me alone. To be in a place of love no matter what was said or done would be training that was far beyond what I knew then.

CHAPTER 20

September to October

1997

Meher Baba, as the Avatar, descends to the level of each individual and has a unique relationship with everyone. To seekers, He is the Goal; to some He is the Divine Mother; to some He is the Father; while to others He is the Friend, the Companion; and to His lovers, HE is the Eternal Beloved. But invariably, He used the language of the individual's heart to call each one to Him. . . . And to a few He even appears in divine visions.[1]

Bal Natu

While still in my Villa Ravine apartment in Gainesville, late one afternoon, in my bedroom next to the large screened-porch, both made airy by palm trees, I saw a vision of Meher Baba coming through the doorway. He carried me in His arms to where Mehera sat on the floor with her legs to one side, then lowered me to lie across her lap. He was the father, she the mother, and her lap my bassinet. Later, I would see this as my arrival into the Meher Baba family.

By September, the decision to go to Meherabad had been made, but I had only enough money for a down payment on a reserved ticket for November. I needed my home in Massachusetts to sell in time to make the final payment. While I waited in Florida, my dad, from his home in Rhode Island, watched the progress of a Congressional bill that would allow homeowners fifty-five and older to qualify for a one-time home sale without paying a property gains tax. I had turned fifty-five in February.

My home in Longmeadow had been under repair for a year, including the installation of a new roof. As soon as my father let me know that the bill had passed, I hired painters for the outside of the house, and on the day they started, two things happened: a friend put out the For Sale sign and a young couple bought my house. They had been driving down Birnie Road in a last effort to find a home before giving up and looking in another town. My home caught their eye.

By October, I had a ticket to India partially paid, my house was sold but the final payment not yet made, and David returned from Wales. It was the only time that he came for three workshops in one year. As our group lay on the floor for a long meditation with directions to see our life purpose, I anticipated seeing (and reading) a paragraph in inner vision, but was surprised for there to be only two words, "Love Messenger," that I very quickly read. Now, nine months after my first January 1997 reading from David, this time he told me to think of the man with the little

black book (Jesse) as a kind of lion who would first see me as a
poor, defenseless lamb, but, as there was a distance between us, I
would be safe. Then I would be seen as a hyena who was his ene-
my, followed by an irritating monkey, and finally as another kind
of lion, like himself. No time frame was given. A final clue was,
"He's the most important man on the planet to you." By then, I
had begun to have dim memories of previous lives, and thinking
back to my urge to put my arm around Jesse's waist as we had
stood by his back field fence, looking at his neighbor's horses, I
realized that I had been experiencing soul recognition.

I became aware that every effort David made was intended to
cause me to see differently, which, after six years, would bring
me to the point where I would move to Meherabad. Proceeding
through my training, I seemed to understand David at a deeper level without questioning—and that what he told me, which
might make no sense in the moment, would at a later time. Perhaps my years of writing with metaphors caused my acceptance
of his. Our relationship was a pattern repeated many times, and
what he told me I didn't share with anyone. When I eventually
moved, I sent all of my recordings to friends at Meher Center and
took my readings to the town dump. They held valuable information about me, but I preferred to remember what I naturally
would and let the rest go.

"It's like this," David had said one day. "You're with everybody
fishing on one side of the boat and you go to the other side where
nobody is. 'Look at all the fish!' you say," and he'd leaned back,
showing me through the look on his face the surprise I was going to find. Another time he said, "You're no good to God unless
you're happy." Given my circumstances, I didn't think I qualified,
but determined to change, I came up with an image to help me
remember a time when I did feel happy to prompt me for when
I felt unhappy. I imagined myself on South Village Beach at
low tide with tiny open pockets of sand, scurrying fiddler crabs,

seagulls circling above, and my feet happily splashing through little waves rolling and receding, their bluish gray deepening under dissolving rims of foam, as sunset cast a shimmering path to collected bits of shells.

DISCOVERING

•

CHAPTER 21

Living Alone and Yet Together

1997–1998

True love is no game of the faint-hearted and the
weak; it is born of strength and understanding.[1]

Meher Baba

Once my Longmeadow house was sold, for the next 18 years, whenever I was in America, with plans to be in Florida, I lived in a small farmhouse where a border of pine, hickory, and live oak trees surrounded the field with its angled row of dogwood and redbud, and a grassy path bordering the fenced garden led to an aging pear orchard. In front of the meditation studio, two live oaks grew close together, with one-third of their leaves intermingled and two-thirds separate and distinct against the sky. During those 18 years, I was being taught that love is not what I believed it to be. My changing required that I let go of everything I thought was right, and in these trees—alone and yet together—I found a metaphor for this new love.

At the time I had met Jesse in May before he left on sabbatical I was living in a too big, too expensive apartment. Remembering that he told me he might want to rent his place, as he would be away for six months, I had found a driveway off the lime rock road, wondering as I drove through woods if I had turned at the right mailbox. Blackie, an abandoned, mistrustful dog who was welcomed at the food bowl with Jesse's other dogs but who fended for herself when he was away, lay in the front yard with six round, fat, black or caramel-colored puppies. As I walked through the tall grass to the porch, in those early few moments, I had stood still in a theater of humming insects and known this was my home—and that the thought was totally inappropriate. Nonetheless, I'd felt undeniable contentment, as in coming home, and an unquenchable longing to stay. My move to the farm happened that first day in September when I drove into the yard, not in late October when I brought my things out from town.

Surprised to see the front door open, and stepping inside the back sliding glass door, I paused, looking around, and noticed a note on the table and a mound of mail, some of which had slid to the floor. I had wanted the farm to be vacant, but while it didn't look lived in, an open carton of milk in the refrigerator told me that someone had been there. I left my own note, asking that if need be, could I store my things. Then, as the puppies looked old enough to be weaned, I emptied some of the milk into a bowl, hoping that it wouldn't be missed.

Considering Blackie would need to raid garbage cans—upsetting neighbors who might call the pound—or kill rabbits and squirrels, I decided to return the next day to find homes for her litter, and perhaps an answer to my note. Not knowing how to catch scared puppies, I put a bowl of milk in the pantry, leaving the outside door open, while I hid behind the pantry wall, scarcely breathing, holding a string tied to the doorknob. One by one, a puppy suspiciously nosed its way in. Pulling the door closed as quietly as possible, I scooped up each one, depositing it in an empty bedroom where I'd put a bowl of water and newspapers on a scuffed, painted floor. By the time I'd caught all of them, except one, I was soaked in pee—wet *and* smelly, but smiling. Needing a dry top, I opened drawers until I found Jesse's tee shirts and took out the oldest one to put on. Now presentable, I walked the lime rock road until I found a man who told me that his wife took their kittens to the Winn Dixie. I got directions and once there put the five puppies in a shopping cart. Not knowing anything about them, when someone told me they were a nice Labrador-Chow mix, I passed that on to the next person, until all five were taken.

Back at the farm, the last puppy had been the only one to approach me for an exploratory sniff. With determination, I now chased him, grabbing his hind legs as he dove into a dugout under a big rock. Getting squirted with stool this time, I borrowed another tee shirt. At Winn Dixie again, I waited with this final puppy, alone in the cart, feeling a growing sadness. When an older lady said she'd have to go ask her husband before taking him, I waited for her to leave, then picked up my puppy, and ran to the car. We went directly to the town vet, who gave him shots and was helpful with a plan. He would stay with her when I left for Meherabad, getting plenty of attention from her attendants and be outside with her companion dogs in the grassy exercise yard. On questioning, she had smiled when I told her to remember "bow-wow," when pronouncing his name. Bhauji and I spent all our time together, as I carried him like a baby, and when I drove he licked my leg.

My apartment manager didn't like that I had a pet as they weren't allowed, so I'd continued searching for a smaller place, but my efforts turned up nothing, until one last possibility. My departure date was November 11, and by now it was late October. Calling the realtor to sign papers, I felt helpless upon hearing that she had rented the three-room house two hours earlier. Now I wondered if I could move my things into the farm, and with the thought that I could help Jesse—I began cleaning. It was dying in cobwebs and dust. When my inner voice said, "I'm helping you, as he won't," I believed it was a message from Meher Baba. When the crows said, "Hurry up, hurry up," I realized I was to move in without asking Jesse, who might say no. My behavior was totally uncharacteristic, and I didn't look forward to calling him.

Going through the rooms, I looked for his photo, as it had been May when we'd met, and I now had no memory of his appearance. When I did find a worn photo of a man seated with a boy standing beside him, I mistakenly thought the boy was Jesse when younger. The boy in the photo was Jesse's twenty-one-year old son, who finally appeared. Flashing an arresting smile, he listened to my story, and in his relaxed presence we agreed I needed to make a call. Jesse's first reaction was shock, but when I asked on behalf of Meher Baba, he turned amenable, and I heard the answer I had hoped for. Now I brought out my things.

CHAPTER 22

A Pilgrimage

1997–1998

The easiest way to achieve the Goal of Life is to 'leave all and follow Me' through Love. I do not mean that you should leave your house and family and come here! I mean that you be in your house and with your family but love Me as I want you to love Me—love Me above all.[1]

Meher Baba

The money from the sale of my house arrived three days before I needed to make the final payment on my ticket, and I had a letter from Jesse saying that he would meet me in Mumbai with a driver. My travel would include a stop in Germany to see Mother Meera who embodies the Divine Mother; to pilgrims who come for her darshan, she "bestows light upon the soul and answers individual prayers."[2] I had arranged to stay for three evenings of darshan, and following the required etiquette of washing my hair beforehand, I entered a room smaller than I had imagined with chairs in rows on either side of an aisle where Mother Meera came in to sit in front facing us. There was complete silence until the first row of people stood, with only the sound of their bodies moving as they formed a line and one at a time each approached her. By watching I knew what to do when it was time for my row. When I was motioned to her, after I knelt she put her hands on my head, and I put my hands on her feet. Then I looked up and into her eyes, stood, and returned to my seat. When the silent darshan ended, we sat in quiet until she rose and left and then we followed. I felt so thankful to have come, and grateful to Jesse, who had been before, for his suggestion.

For the remainder of my stay in Germany, I was on my own. The small village and the surrounding countryside were quaint, with the next village only a walk away. The air was fresh, and in the village, I bought a loaf of bread in a small shop. I left the country knowing that I had made the right decision.

On my final flight, Mumbai appeared welcoming, as out the window vast orchards of lights appeared indicating its size in the dark. The stern-faced armed guards at Immigration and Customs were scary, and emerging beyond them, I looked apprehensively at a small, dirty, poorly lit waiting room, hoping as I walked that my memory of Jesse would return. Hearing my name spoken quietly, I turned to see a man in a tan safari hat, a soft, long-sleeved white shirt open at the neck, and pale yellow pants who was smiling at me and standing so close that I was inches from bumping into him.

I followed Jesse through the open double doors into the heated 2:00 a.m. night lit by streetlight—a world that looked like a movie set where Humphrey Bogart and Lauren Bacall would appear. His driver waited in the crowd, pressed against the barricades, watching for us. In my excitement, I let go of the stress of the trip, reassuring myself that I carried a thousand dollars, three months' rent for the use of his home.

After a five-minute ride to the Leela Hotel, we waited in a vast lounge with bronze statues and tall potted plants placed for discreet intimacy, where sounds came from a fountain splashing in a circular stairwell amid voices of waiters and early morning revelers. Returning to the car just two hours later after the driver's brief sleep, we started off through the outskirts of Mumbai. Passing homeless people who slept on sidewalks, clusters of men drinking chai under tin sheds or flagging rides in trucks, in the still-dark hour, with a row of traffic climbing up the Western Ghats, we headed southeast then north toward Ahmednagar. Without fully disappearing, my apprehension calmed in the self-confident presence of this man who, I now learned, had first come to Meherabad in 1989. I felt free and ready to take on India.

CHAPTER 23

Adjustment

1997–1998

It is natural that at times you feel 100%
miserable. Be sure that I know everything. When everything goes wrong, the
mind becomes helpless and has to rely
on the heart. These are the moments
when you resign to my will and rely sole-
ly on my help. When you leave all to Me,
I dare not neglect you, and you get relief
from your predicament. I am the Ocean
of Love and Compassion.[1]

Meher Baba

This was a time of adjustment.

Arriving at Meherabad at the end of the monsoon season to a world that was all green, except for earthen paths, sky, and buildings, I felt its enchantment. Housed on the women's side of the residence having three walls of bedrooms facing a courtyard of old trees with character and flowering vines entangled among flowering bushes, I had a bed beside a woman who liked to quietly read. She kept her mosquito netting down, so we spoke little. Called to the office one day, I was surprised to find that I was listed with her last name, which caused me to smile and then correct. I shared that with her, and it seemed to awaken in her a sense of awareness that I had been given her last name as mine. Over the years of her coming for short periods of time, while I continued living here, our friendship gradually became ever closer, until by now I feel her friendship always from Italy.

As I learned of American residents who had been here thirty years, I began to say that I was in Meher Baba's cradle. David had told me that I was of the light and not to pay attention to certain comments, but I felt uncomfortable to miserable from many that I received when I shared some of my past experiences. I thought, "I will never invite anyone here." Others weren't interested in what my experiences had been. Several read a warning from Meher Baba given to a woman mandali on psychic ability and practice. A few listened when I shared then only said to "give it to Baba." I appreciated their kindness.

Finally I found a field that I could go to privately where chin up, holding back tears, I walked through a strip of trees, over a low stonewall (watching for snakes), through a doorway in the tall, thick cacti, and alone, sat on my heels as tears flooded my face, releasing fears that there was something wrong about me. It was a sloping field that I consciously appreciated for its rural beauty, with only a few buildings visible before hills, and for its inspiration to mentally distance my situation from my emotions.

When peace and quiet came, I'd stretch up and head back keeping very still inside as I watched my escape route become a nature walk and my suffering, acceptance.

There also were times of unusual experiences that appeared to occur to persuade me that I was meant to be here. Before I left America, David had told me that Mehera, Meher Baba's beloved, was my constant companion who was with me whenever Meher Baba wasn't. When Jesse gave me a silver-plated cup engraved with "Mehera," calling it my constant companion, wonderingly, I thanked him.

Kneeling by Mehera's shrine close to my leaving, I heard a voice meant as hers say, "You may love, serve, and be devoted to your beloved, but you must always love, serve, and be devoted to my Beloved first." At Meherazad, Meher Baba's residence and the home of His remaining mandali, His closest disciples, I shared her words with Aloba who told me, "You are fortunate from all angles."

Another day when I was momentarily standing inside the threshold, not yet having taken steps to sit down, Meher Baba spoke saying that He was giving my heart "gold milk." I pictured bright, barely-curved strands of gold in milk, and for two years thanked Him, until one morning when I heard "God milk;" He had been patient and creative.

During my pilgrimage, on many days I had taken the Trust bus from Meherabad to Meherazad, an hour away, to wait in lines to say "Jai Baba" and sometimes be hugged by the remaining mandali. Arnavaz was the one for whom I had the greatest feeling. She was also the one to whom Meher Baba had given His warning. On an early trip when I had still been struggling with my place at Meherabad, I had approached her and asked if she would listen. Telling her every detail about myself, I had then waited, apprehensive about her response. Looking at me understandingly, compassionately and lovingly, all she had asked was, "Do you love Baba?"

On the January morning of the day that I was leaving to return to America, I changed my direction away from Meher Baba's shrine, where I added a flower to the garlands each day, and instead headed for the Upper Compound looking for a different flowering bush to pick my one. Only today I would be saying "Good-bye." By the door on the east side of the water tank, tiny, white five-petal flowers of a jasmine bush lit up its green fullness that was draped over wooden posts. As I leaned to pick one, I stopped, for I heard "do not bring a flower for you are my jasmine." Slowly my hand dropped and I straightened, surprised and unsure of what to do. In the quiet of seconds I thought, "How can I go without a flower?" But I turned now and walked to the shrine. Hesitant before the soft glow of the wooden threshold, I stepped over and stood, feeling awkwardly empty-handed, but immediately heard "you do not need a flower for you are my jasmine." Amazed and without words, I kneeled and placed my head on the altar cloth.

CHAPTER 24

A New and Different Life

1998–1999
There lies the fun of the game—to meet
opposition, to face and encounter it...One
can find spirituality only through opposition.[1]
Meher Baba

When I returned to Jesse's farm the first of February, my puppy, older now, was there, and Jesse invited me to stay. It was then that I assertively trapped Blackie, taking her to be altered so she wouldn't need to give birth again. At the vet's, I sat with her on the floor of her cage before and after surgery. Back at the farm, one morning, silent and unseen, she approached me from behind and touched her nose to the back of my knee. Startled by the intimacy, I turned quickly, reaching out my hand, and, amazed, felt her fur brush my fingertips as she shied away. While she stood eyeing me, I saw a royal blue aura undulate along her back, and in sudden soul recognition understood that on the September day that I had driven into the farm, Blackie had been in the front yard with her puppies to evoke my compassion and cause my return.

Now that I had begun to read about Meher Baba I was no longer defining what happened to me as "good" or "bad." But as I wasn't ready to see everything as good, I found my words in "easy-good" or "hard-good." I knew that each experience had a purpose, and how I responded mattered more than what had happened. When I discovered Bhauji leaping at laundry hung between the trees, and on one day tore a hole in Jesse's favorite school tee shirt, I gave a stern "No," folded the shirt carefully in regret for its gaping tear, and pragmatically climbed to tie the rope higher, but then changed to a smile for his endearing mischief. I could change, but not my playful dog.

The farm was all varnished pine and my room so small that I had to kneel on the end of the handmade cedar bed to get into the closet. I loved its west-facing window taking up half the wall, where in the morning I propped up pillows to look out at the roughly mowed yard and the trees, where birds and animals moved and leaves were shifting. I could see the end of the sand driveway that left the woods and turned to ruts in scraggly grass where to the right pink and white azaleas clumped around a tree and to the left stood the end posts of Muscodine grapes before curving in a wide circle around an old canvas shed to stop at the painted, dark brown deck off the kitchen. From there you could drive anywhere out to the unmown field, except near the septic tank under the Rose of Sharon.

This was the first time I'd lived in seclusion among abundant grasses. I explored the woods, following the boundary fences. Feeling peaceful inside the farm that sat in the middle of the long field between patterned rows of planted trees and ones placed by nature, I looked out and met my new family—scrambling, squabbling birds at the feeder I hung, wheeling hawks, grazing deer and wild turkey, a passing fox partially visible, and a steadily crawling, long-term resident gopher tortoise on its routes.

My first April, I tacked a laminated photo of Meher Baba to a garden fence post. He was young, and His hair looked like two large, long, and soft curly-hair "dog ears." Below I had typed, "God is omnipresent, and the one who calls out sincerely to Him never fails to be heard and to receive His help."[2] Two weeks went by. Then one day I opened the gate to weed and saw the photo had changed—rose pink columns as soft-edged as clouds framed the triangle of His hair and in the lightest percentage of pastel splotched His right cheek and chin. Perplexed, as I had worked in graphic arts, I stared, unable to imagine rainwater causing black ink to wash to rose, until it dawned on me this was Meher Baba deepening my belief.

That spring of 1998, when Jesse asked if I wanted to prune the overgrowth of grape vines, I agreed. The work was hard and my pruning looked more like a butchering, but I enjoyed the work outside and decided to do more. Jesse was still at the school where he taught, and for some forgotten reason, I started on the jasmine bush, not thinking to wait and ask his permission. It was in a corner on the back of the farm where the screened porch adjoined his bedroom, the corner lost behind the full-bodied bush, its fragrance emanating from the tiny, white flowers dotting the mass of greenery. Long, small-leaved, and pliant branches gracefully spread in every direction until they found a rough bit of board to attach to.

Having owned property for years, I was accustomed to doing what I wanted. I didn't know his jasmine was the green jewel of the farm, or that he was thoroughly imbued with love for it. Later, from years of observing him, I would understand his master's degree in horticulture as a statement, but not the truth—that he was the tree itself as well as the grower. So, in enthusiasm lacking respect, I balanced on a chair and trimmed the edges of the bush and kept trimming.

I was reading in the living room that night when he suddenly came from his bedroom, his voice a storm of shock, anger, and blame as he told me that his jasmine had been butchered! Immobile, with my back pressed to the sofa, I listened in horror to his description, never having felt such pain coming from someone whose heart was torn open by damage to a bush. My wanting to help was a weak defense, and my apology ineffectual. I felt remorse in a way that I hadn't ever felt it before, and while I had a brief thought—I had lost a *husband,* and this was only a *bush*—I realized that this had no bearing on the present situation. From a new place of awareness, I kept quiet. I knew that I was to listen and not fail at silence.

After he quieted and left, I took my keys and, although it was after eight, drove forty minutes to a home improvement center, where I bought six jasmine plants from the garden shop. That was all I could think to do, to offer more than words of apology and to ease my guilt. In the dark, with light from stars and shafts out the farm windows, I sorrowfully left the pots by the porch. They were never planted. Yellow, not white, their sort already climbed with wild profusion in the nearby southern pines. They didn't hold the memories of his damaged jasmine.

September was my eighth month living at the farm. Initially

I had felt relieved that I had a place to stay; then I had discovered how much I wanted to stay. Autumn here was so different from that of my New England childhood. I watched the varying browns and occasional yellow and red leaves as I undertook the farm chores. I was in a two-year period where I'd been told by David not to work. Questioned why I couldn't give readings, he had answered that I should tell my friends that I was on sabbatical. Other than errands, my limited time away from the farm was a weekly ministerial ordination class and meditation group of five women and two men, who also met with David. Each week, I shared small news—that I had hung out laundry, been to the dump, or was raking.

Old washing machines and refrigerators lined the back of the farm, and an abandoned van parked in the woods had debris to the ceiling. Looking for helpful work I could do, I decided to make trips to a landfill. What I lacked for muscle, I made up for by using leverage and gravity to wrestle the outworn appliances into the back of my older Saab. Then I emptied the van too. Each time I drove off was an adventure. My self-appointed jobs were improving the farm and increasing my feelings of helpfulness.

For days, I raked leaves under the two biggest live oaks that shaded the front of the farm. Where the ground was more dirt than grass, the raking was easy, but the garden was a distance behind the farm and my arm and shoulder muscles ached from dragging the big, over-stuffed, plastic trash can. I raked because I liked the work. I raked because it would be useful to have the leaves brought to the garden, to dig into the soil. When I was done, garbage cans of leaves were now in mounds for compost.

Sometimes Jesse thanked me for the work I did. This time he didn't, although I knew he had noticed. In his silence, and not wanting to ask for appreciation, I took a new step. I told Meher Baba what I had done, and each day continued talking to *Him* about my day's work. I felt better. Inner appreciation was reliable, outer was not, and that was what I needed to learn. When my efforts were spoken of enthusiastically, that would please me, but I no longer had an expectation of thanks.

One afternoon, I wrote a prayer that became my constant friend for two years. Kneeling in the meditation studio before a photo of Baba, where I'd come in need of a view other than jealousy, I repeated, "Meher Baba, I'm feeling hurt. No one and nothing has caused my hurt. Thank you for taking it away."

If a doorbell had its wire cut, pressing the bell wouldn't cause it to ring. That is how I lived for the first two years, 1998 and 1999, facing Jesse's sudden mood swings and observing, more often than getting upset or entangled. My body had been changed to be like that bell with its wire cut. By the third year, David had told me I could stay or leave, but if I stayed Jesse's unkindness would get harder for me to bear, and now I did feel his unkindness when it occurred, but because of the two-year hiatus, I had a buffer-space that, if not infallible, gave me enough emotional restraint for most situations. In grudging admiration and reluctant humor, I recognized my helplessness to change this and accepted Meher Baba's method of training me and my need for a lot of practice. I came to know that pain and peace together nurtured plainly-seen improvement.

PEACH ORCHARD

I could see him in the orchard—well, not all of him. I could see his legs on the ladder balanced on the uneven field. The rest of him had disappeared into the branches of the peach tree. The next time I looked, he was standing on the ground, elbow bent, his cupped hand holding something. His hand moved toward his mouth. Inside the farmhouse, drying my hands on a dishtowel, I tasted peach juice in my mouth. My chin felt wet as he brought his hand to his mouth again. Peaches sat in a row across the sink windowsill, their yellow jackets covered with fuzzy pink splotches. Was he after riper, sweeter peaches? These were hard. Not as sweet as they would get. But he was hungry for peaches and had been eating them. I turned back to the orchard. He had disappeared—again—the third time up, I counted. I caught sight of his hand twisting off a peach. As he brought it to his mouth without climbing down the ladder, my hands felt sticky.

PJC 2000

DEEPENING

CHAPTER 25

A Ministry of Counseling

1999–2002

I may give you more, much more than
you expect, or maybe nothing, and that
nothing may prove to be everything...[1]

Meher Baba

During the earlier writing of the final chapter on Stephen, I had originally titled it, "A Seed for Journey's End," knowing at the time that something about the ending of my journey with Stephen was a seed for my future. The seed would germinate as my ministerial ordination. Meher Baba writes, "I have come to sow the seed of love in your hearts,"[2] reaching out to me before I was aware of Him.

In February 1998, having returned to the farm in Florida from my ten-week Christmas pilgrimage to Meherabad, I was eager to join the first group of an Alliance of Divine Love interfaith ministerial ordination class at Seraphim Center, beginning in April, attracted by its motto of "The Greatest Degree of Love." But I needed to travel to see family. So, taking the textbook, I had completed the reading and exercises while away from the class, and started in June.

We were ordained the following December, and by January 1999, I had signed up for my ministerial internship, choosing the Gainesville Hospice. The building, off a woodsy turn on 39th Avenue, was spacious and airy, with art on the walls and outside along the walkways, a skirting of flowers. Homey and only discreetly medical, it was limited to residents with a doctor's prognosis of six months to live. My friend was the chef. I had been visiting him for months, using the kitchen as a home base to become familiar and comfortable with the rooms and the idea of volunteering. After the three-day training, I began a weekly schedule of two hours a week, immediately assigned to Maheshi, a devotee of Gurumayi. Having Ani Tuzman for a friend, who I write of in "Finding My Niche," and who was a writer for Gurumayi, I had even visited her ashram in upstate New York. Gurumayi, a Siddha guru in the lineage of Swami Muktananda, well known in the west, teaches the Siddhas' message that the experience of divine consciousness is attainable in this human body. "[She] points us back inside ourselves where this state is both possible and attainable.["](3) I easily slipped into greeting Maheshi, whose name was also one of Shiva's, with "Jai Gurumayi," and over the next year and a half thus fully completed my one-year internship.

Having my service work in place, I was ready to focus my attention on my private counseling ministry. Following a January Sunday service at Seraphim Center, Reverend Bob, the minister, founder, and my ordination teacher had asked me to follow him to see rooms he'd just rented for our use. When he opened the first door, I saw two big windows facing north and west in the diagonal corner, with bushes and vines in view. The room was square, airy, and bright. I chose that one and added two maple rockers facing each other across a small table that held a wooden mallet and chime, along with a rose quartz heart, a green stone, and a black one—all smooth for holding. Framed pictures of Meher Baba and American Indian art gave the walls personality, and under the desk-glass, photos of Mother Teresa and other holy people and a blue and white bird family offered a message in response to the curious glance. I filled the room with toys and art materials, as I had ideas about how to illustrate emotional situations in a different way.

Now I was ready, but had no clients. I'd had a session with David on de-cording that was explained as beneficially healing in an article in *Touchstone,* a local New Age paper: "De-cording identifies damaging mental concepts and deep-seated emotions that with a minimum of discussion can be understood and corrected. By focusing on clearing out useless misconceptions, the mind and body become more relaxed and thus freer and better energized to use existing guidance, intuition, and love to rediscover the innate joy in life that comes with a clear and tranquil mind and heart.["](4)

For an hour, David took me through the steps, giving directions, asking me for names, and telling me people and beliefs I was to work with. Toward the end, he added Meher Baba, saying that I was carrying betrayal from my life with Jesus, and Meher Baba would now teach me who He was. I felt humbled by this. When David ended, he told me I had done de-cording in many lifetimes, and would be able to do it with others. First I had to practice on my own, requiring every morning for two months my determined search for those people and situations where I had conflict. I counted a total beyond sixty before stopping but afterward would return to the process when needed.

By late January, I had made a flyer offering four de-cording sessions. Of the twenty people who came, all except one were able to follow my directions and feel their body and emotions relax as unneeded cordings dissolved. One of these people asked to return for regular counseling and remained for a year and a half, becoming the cornerstone as others followed, bringing my practice to life.

My office was a surprise of newsprint drawing pads, fat crayons, big markers, Taos drum, turtle rattle, yellow pail with a nerf football and soap bubbles, hula hoop, jump rope, small girl and boy dolls with happy, sad, shy, confused, or angry faces, a family of stuffed animals, each a different animal to represent family differences, and children's books all gathered and waiting to help people look at emotional health in a new and creative way. Talking didn't necessarily bring change; but having a person repeatedly catch a nerf football I tossed toward a lap while I repeatedly let it bounce to the floor brought questioning. What I said was that as children we caught everything thrown our way, but as adults we could choose. I wanted people to leave my office thinking about a nerf ball colored like confetti rather than their drama, knowing it was a safe space, and that my way of helping was different from their earlier experiences in counseling. Change would come from within, not from without.

I began each session with the chime tapped three times by the client facing me then quietly spoke these words, "I ask that the greatest degree of love be present for all concerned, that I be a clear and accurate channel of information, and that we remember all healing comes from a greater source within." I said I was not clinically trained, but worked through my heart, and could only give invitations for what I was practicing. I spoke of kindness for oneself, trying what I offered, and if any small change occurred to feel grateful and return. I had a clown in my heart whose job was to dilute seriousness, and I allowed about fifteen minutes for hearing what the concern was then nudged the conversation toward my playful approach to new understanding. My true purpose was to teach that everyone is God, so I affirmed without blame, tapping into the inherent love in each heart as the true source of empowerment. This meant becoming one hundred percent responsible. My intention remained unspoken, as those words would have been received by the intellect, and my goal was to reach a person's subconscious, where healing answers indirectly waited.

The morning my first client arrived I had been wondering what I would say, but my concern was short-lived. Following my opening comment, surprised, she said, "How did you know what I was thinking?" This became the pattern. My words eased each seeker to feel known and to willingly talk. The different views I offered came from higher guidance, causing me to think of a puppeteer above doing the work and keeping my ego from feeling important.

What a client thought was the problem was usually not what I saw. When a circumstance was described in the present, I could find its origin, unresolved, in the past. My insight would evoke surprise, and shift the focus from blaming to an inner search for answers. If, referring to being unable to change a situation, I was asked, "Why can't I?" I would raise my right hand high, saying, "This is your level of achievement in many areas." Then, holding my left hand slightly above my lap I added, "This is your emotional level. You are in kindergarten, and I'm in third grade, but I am far enough ahead to help you." Then I asked when the person had learned addition, fractions, or *calculus*—that brought laughter, as most of us had not made it that far. But my following question, quietly spoken as I watched, caused a searching look to appear. "When did you study your emotions, anger? When did you learn about yourself and relationships?" As none of us had, I answered, "We can't fail at what we have not been taught. Now we can learn," including myself in that mix.

When I took out the giant, hot-pink soap bubble jar, I heard, "I haven't blown bubbles in years!" As the soapy globes floated, I'd say that most people saw soap bubbles, but to one of the members of my writing group, they were "the iridescent pearls of children." I wanted to evoke a feeling of wonder from a childlike view. Life is perception and perception can change. In fear, our tendency is to forget this. Anger over a divorce can be viewed in a new way by changing it to a positive feeling about the divorce having a helping purpose for the one left as well as the one leaving. Watching the hula hoop circle around hips, I asked the person to stand still and let it drop, then said, "We twist ourselves out of shape trying to please others, but dropping the hoop means making our own decisions." When I opened an early reader book to a double page where children played hide and seek, pointing to several of them running away close to the edges, I said, "In certain ways, some of us never returned to home base at 'All-y, all-y in free,' and instead we remained children hiding within, unobserved or misunderstood." Our bodies grew into adults and we unknowingly behaved inappropriately, not from our adult common sense but from the incomplete child needing to grow competent and responsible.

My decision to change how I related to men helped in my counseling. I had settled on having three things about any one man be important—and the rest, I would manage. At one appointment, a woman came with a complaint that her husband had mowed the lawn but had not put back the flowerpots. Leaning forward, I said, incredulously, "He mowed the lawn. He actually mowed the lawn. That's great. He mowed the lawn and—didn't move the flowerpots back. They can stay until he does, or they can just stay, or you can move them. He actually ... mowed the lawn!" I stopped and, without moving, kept my eyes on her. She looked at me as I waited expectantly. Then suddenly, she relaxed in her chair, smiled, and we both laughed. She understood I wasn't making fun of her. She was ready and willing to see that change didn't have to do with flowerpots, but with how she looked at them.

My goal was to have everyone be able to counsel him or herself. While situations had different details, underneath were principles of truth. I had only a few tools in my box. One belief was that everyone is always doing his or her best. Even the slightest change in a situation was reason to celebrate. I validated people's thoughts and feelings as their perceptions, without blaming, criticizing, or judging. They'd been told, "You should have known better" or "I can't believe at your age you did that." I'd stopped using *should* in 1986 and replaced it with *could*. I didn't *have* to do anything, although there were always consequences. It had been an early step in separating who I was from what others wanted me to be. I understood that unkind comments revealed information about the speaker rather than the one spoken about. I used the mirror principle of others reflecting me, knowing that when I remained neutral, a situation was not about me, but if I felt emotional, the issue was mine. Alone, I did not know what was best for each client. I relied on guidance added to my creative approach. The view didn't always follow socially acceptable behavior—as when one man told me he didn't want to visit a nursing home, I'd said, "Don't," believing he needed support to do what he truly wanted, not merely what was expected of him. He could decide later if he'd been right or wrong, and accept any consequence, but he would have found the courage to make *his* decision—regardless of other views. Another tool I had was my awareness that synchronicity exists between what we need to learn and what happens, even if we don't always recognize the inherent harmony. Life to me is more than a series of coincidences or accidents. One night, reflecting on my work while driving home in only traffic hum, between the distractions of towns, my inner voice surprised me, saying I would know shame the next day. It was not a word I used, although I had recently read that it differs from guilt to the extent that it sees the person as bad, rather than the behavior. Mid-morning the next day, having forgotten the message, I was vacuuming, when emotion so strong washed through me, I had to sit down on the sofa. Scenes pushed away since I was a young girl and teenager surfaced unbidden, until I realized that what I was feeling was *shame*: I felt sad and empty, angry and weak. I hurt. I felt misunderstood and "ashamed" that I hadn't known better. As I allowed the memories to ebb, I began talking aloud with words of understanding and acceptance. I released a little sigh, and my body slouched back. I felt my slight smile of wonder, then a bigger sigh. As my chest heaved out and in, the smile became a grin. I felt a kind of quiet. Through the releasing of that secret pain, I felt wiser and more experienced about the hiding capacity of shame. Mine had been with me for fifty years. Now I felt grateful. The next week, when a client came who was feeling shame, I could help.

One morning, I had left the farm with enough time to arrive at my office five minutes before my first appointment. Starting my car, I backed up—and lodged my back right wheel on a protruding rock. Frustrated, I got out and put boards under the tire. That failing, I attempted to lift the car. When I couldn't, in defeat I started to walk away and then suddenly dropped to my knees and pounded the ground, hollering, "Why is this happening to me? I'm going to be late!" Moments later, I sat up with complete inner calm and said to myself, in adult appraisal, "I'm having a temper tantrum. This is what it is like." I didn't remember ever having one, and had only heard others lose control. Standing up, I went in, phoned my road help agency, then the center, and patiently waited for professional rescue.

Through four years of my intuitive counseling, I asked, "Do you love yourself when you're angry?" Each person answered no. I practiced loving myself when hurt, angry, or jealous, when I had unkind thoughts or words, and especially when I acted from my fears, and I repeatedly sang Jai Josef's "I love myself the way I am, there's nothing I need to change."⁵ When I asked a client, "If there were a hundred weeds and one flower, what would you look at?" and "If there were a hundred flowers and one weed, what?" My answer was, "Keep your attention on the flower—or the flowers." Where we put our thoughts is where our energy goes. "Kind words, kind echoes," my sister called it.

In August 2002, I heard my inner voice instruct me to do no more readings. Then a client told me that she had dreamed that two people were being considered to go to India, and I was the one chosen, as I had the right abilities. Laughing, I asked her to dream the date, and told her I thought Meher Baba was calling her, too. Next, I received two emails from David, one week apart. The first said that it was time to return to Samadhi and the second added "sooner rather than later," as a window of opportunity that was open would be closing and it would be a shame for me to miss it and have to repeat my progress up to where I was three lifetimes in the future. My final persuasion was hearing my inner voice say, "No more counseling. No more fee charging." How could I support myself? The obvious answer was, I couldn't. I must be supposed to move to India.

Three years earlier, at Meherabad, I had recounted my occult experiences to Meredith Moon, a Jungian and Transpersonal therapist, and a longtime Baba lover, believing that with her knowledge of archetypes and symbols, she would be comfortable listening and have a helpful response. She paid attention for a half hour then answered in three minutes, telling me she believed that in the future Meher Baba would take me on a great leap. At that time, my abilities would disappear. How would I feel? My answer came easily. I had never asked for my occult abilities, and used them, offered to God, with my best talent. When they left, that was fine. The "leap" had later been my destined move.

My answer was right.

My occult abilities meant I had inner vision, inner hearing, and inner knowing. During the editing of the book, Meredith wrote to me, "Baba uses them [occult abilities] to bring us into spiritual realities but then because the ego becomes attached to specialness (a grave hindrance on the path) He takes them away, allowing their importance to fade in the deepening journey of love."[6]

My coming departure upset my clients but had its own gift. I gave a one-month intensive training to those who had become ordained Alliance of Divine Love ministers, as I was, and were interested in continuing the True Self groups or offering counseling. Of the nine women and one man who attended, three kept my office open another two years under their leadership. Eventually I talked with a woman who had attended one of those True Self groups, and she was radiant in her description.

CHAPTER 26

True Self:
Inner Child – Inner Parent

1999–2002

The needs that weren't being met as a child
kept me from realizing who I was as an adult.
I... grabbed a hunk of clay and... mashing
this clay... I was so angry, and slowly it
faded and I... made a hummingbird. All this
anger, ...I don't have it anymore. I could release it without holding it in to explode later.

John (a client)

During my first year of counseling, a woman I was meeting for the first time came the day before I was to leave for five weeks in India. We had the same last name, and she told me that she thought this was significant. Because my coming absence upset her, I agreed to stay for a longer session, during which she told me that her father (a faculty member) had called her "stupid." She obviously wasn't—her intellect and her education were evident, but in her own mind, the label had stuck.

Handing her a big newsprint pad, I asked her to draw a table where she and her father sat with a bowl of beef stew. I had her add a voice bubble, and told her to write in big letters, "You're stupid." She waited, not knowing my point. I asked her the difference of how old she'd been then and her age now, then told her she'd been stewing about this insult for that many years. In my pause...she got it. At the end of our time, she said that she had a regular therapist and a support group, but she had never worked this way before. When I saw her again after I returned from India, she showed me a book on the use of non-dominant writing and drawing as therapy whose author she had called in California, only to learn there were no facilitators of the method in Florida. I thumbed through it, considered my experience leading writing groups, and that I had myself once kept a drawing journal for two years—and told her that I might be able to help.

The next day I bought *Recovery of Your Inner Child*[1] by Lucia Capacchione and tried the technique of non-dominant hand drawing that uses the dominant hand for the adult voice and the non-dominant hand for the inner child's voice. Opening to the first exercise, I took the nearest piece of paper, and following directions promptly used my left hand to draw me, in fourth grade, catching pollywogs at a pond on the far end of a field my girlfriends and I biked to. Looking at the slightly awkward lines, I remembered the girl I had been, who loved nature. That first drawing, made on light-blue-lined notebook paper (and still with me) was my final reason to start an inner child group. After more than a year, I ended it—we hadn't yet finished the book, but the group meetings had succeeded in helping people change, and I knew my next step.

In the second year, now calling this group, "True Self: Inner Child – Inner Parent," I put together a seventy-page study notebook of weekly reading assignments along with information sheets on the real and co-dependent self as well as songs and poems. We would finish in ten weeks, and the group could be offered three times a year, at night. I added a cover, drawn by Megan in 1980 when she was in the second grade, of a mother rabbit standing and holding her baby rabbit, facing her. The mother's look of love and concern conveyed how I wanted everyone's inner parent and child to be.

One night at the farm, when I'd been looking at stars, saying the words to the childhood lullaby, "Twinkle, twinkle, little star, how I wonder what you are," I remembered poet and artist Margaret Robison years ago speaking out of her work as an art teacher, telling me that her job was not to teach a teenager who was meeting with her but to help her discover who she was. I knew under those stars that this was the song I wanted to use to begin my group each night.

At each workshop, limited to six women and men, we began by choosing a small, wooden star on a pipe cleaner, three stars knotted together in a crown, or a greeting card with a star, which we waved singing "Twinkle, Twinkle, Little Star," with a variation on the theme changing it to, "Twinkle, twinkle, little star, How I wonder 'who' you are." We wrote, drew, and shared what happened, sang Jai Josef's "I Love Myself the Way I Am," and line-danced to Willie Nelson's "On the Sunny Side of the Street." We ended by standing in a circle swinging our joined hands and singing, "Row, row, row your boat gently down the stream... life is but a dream...life is peaches and cream."

I said that our parents had, in many cases, made us what they wanted rather than helped us to discover who we were. They were not to be blamed, and now our opportunity was for each of us to discover our own selves, with emotional maturing as the core goal. In the exercises, I dredged up my hidden hurt and wrote new endings. What was painful became exciting by new awareness. I remembered a day in junior high school when I had hidden my tears and pretended I was fine, when really I was scared. I didn't have the adult words—betrayed and humiliated—for how I felt. After I biked home and told my mother, she said it was nothing to get upset about—so I had buried my hurt.

When my inner child showed up in an exercise, she told me her name was Abbe. In response to my new understanding, I uncovered those feelings and wrote to Abbe that I felt sad this had happened, and that I hadn't been ready to understand how ashamed she had felt that day. Finishing the exercise, I felt lighter and freer.

In one of Abbe's drawings, she drew a horse with blue lines in the foreground of her bedroom where she is lying on her bed reading. Her hair is orange, her pants blue, and the walls deep pink. Her words were written with my left hand.

Abbe: I read the Black Stallion and I read it in my pink bedroom.

Me: And how did you feel reading that book?

Abbe: I felt all by myself and alone. I was inside myself inside my body.
I was riding the black stallion.

And in my favorite picture of hers, the sky is yellow down to three flowers in unmown grass, where only the bottoms of two big feet and two smaller feet, drawn in orange lines, are sticking straight up.

Me: Abbe, is God real?

Abbe: Dear Mumsie
        How silly of you to ask. Can you make the bird fly
        the cricket sing the chocolate in the chocolate milk.
        Did you design me as your baby.
        Oh Mumsie just breathe and you will know
        God is real.
        Love you
        Abbe

Surprising me eight years later while editing this chapter, Abbe showed up—something was scaring her. I listened and told her that she was safe, then asked her if she'd like to grow up. She answered Yes and told me that the two high pony tails I was wearing because of the heat were her idea. I invited her for a walk up the hill, and the two of us went out, ponytails swinging, headed for the path through the tamarinds to morning prayers, looking for birds to identify on the way.

As weeks passed, I observed that the women and men who came to a group as well as for counseling sessions made more progress than those clients who came only for counseling. By participating in more activities purposefully chosen for the emotional discovery level of a child, they effectively made contact with that aspect most needing to grow.

"There was something missing in my regular therapy—that was ... faith.... Before you can work with other people, you have to love yourself.... Now that I've been in touch with my inner child, before I make any major decisions, I always contact my inner child."

—A. (a client)

My parents had raised me for what they thought was right for me, but rather than growing up into my own self separate from them, able to make decisions from within myself, instead I grew up pleasing them. I did make many decisions, but there were significant opportunities missed for emotional maturing from a young age on.

Beginning with spiritual training in my late forties, I entered a learning curve that intensified in my early fifties, was aided by intuitively guiding clients in my counseling practice as I learned with them, and from which I continued to gradually build a foundation of practice for emotional understanding of new values for myself—and others. Each improvement I made in relating to another I had first found rewarding for me.

ORANGE

One

I watch this orange as a child,
my chin below the counter,
my mother twisting each
orange half on the merry-go-
round of a curved glass dish.
Juice rises and flecks of pulp
float on an orange sea.

ORANGE

Two

I hold this orange as a woman.
My fingernails spade up pith
undressing the thready girdle.
My thumb plunges down
the white well. My tongue
anticipates a sweet tide
as juice jewels jump,
each segment sweet
in my mouth.

PJC 1994

CHAPTER 27

Jesus

1950 − CONTINUING
The Lord is my shepherd; I shall not want.
   He maketh me to lie down in green pastures:
   he leadeth me beside the still waters....
(Ps. 23: 1-2)
David, a shepherd, later a King

•

Compared to my feeling the presence of God as Meher Baba in my life now, intimately talking to Him, aware that He cares for me and guides my life, I do not remember any such awareness of God as a child or a young adult, or not even as a mother raising daughters. I remember my father specifically pointing out that our church had a cross behind the minister's pulpit, not on the altar, and his referring to Jesus as "a good man."

My bedtime prayer, recited each night, as I related earlier, was more about comforting myself because I was alone in the dark than it was about speaking to God. In my room, I liked hearing the church bells' chiming on Sunday mornings and afterwards walking home with my dad holding my hand. Following my Sunday school classes, in my teen years, while I listened to sermons during church, I didn't learn about living with God. I do remember being moved by singing the Lord's Prayer, but it was by the feeling of my body being filled with music. Just one song reached my heart, because its words were of nature, "Morning Has Broken"—"Morning has broken like the first morning, blackbird is calling like the first bird."

Many years later, Paul and I, living in Western Massachusetts, learned of Rev. Thomas Ahlburn at the First Unitarian Church of Providence on Benevolent Street in Rhode Island, and for a period of time our family went across the state each Sunday to hear him. I mention him because of his reputation as an excellent speaker, and this is how I understood my church experience then—about ideas, not living with God as a part of my life.

Moving ahead to 1989, a time of attending support groups, I went to hear a speaker at an Episcopal church during an afternoon group meeting, as the announced presentation had sounded possibly helpful for me. But when he had finished and we stood to go, the congregants of the church left wishing one another, "God be with you" and I left clearly frightened by so many repetitions of those words, and especially of the word God.

And yet, just a year and a half later, by what I now call grace, I felt my heart open—not immediately after joining the East Long-meadow *A Course in Miracles* group, but soon after. There, at the weekly *Course* meetings, I experienced the simplicity of learning that there are aspects of life (love, harmony) that cannot be taken away because they are within, while others can be taken away (marriage, career) because they are without. Gradually, my heart and my mind began to work together. I was able to hear truth as I hadn't been able to before. Through this new understanding of life, I began to accept that there was a way to the peace of God that I could follow.

Twenty-three years after my two years of attending *Course* meetings, I sat down happily with Judy Ebeling, who had been one of the co-leaders on my very first night. Judy asked me if I remembered that on that first night, I had told her there was one word I had a problem with. When Judy had asked me, "What word?" I'd answered, "God." My hours in those studies along with my new practices had initiated a conscious spiritual journey.

Simultaneous with my beginning *A Course in Miracles,* I had begun seeing visions, including visions of Jesus, which I have written about in "Early Occult Experiences." Living with Stephen made Jesus real to me...by learning how he lived with Jesus—Stephen resting his head in his hands, his elbows propped on my kitchen table, saying simply, "Jesus," as I watched from across the room. This gesture of complete faith was in moments when he felt a need for help beyond what he could provide for himself. Stephen's relationship with Jesus was so steadfast that simply by my proximity, seeds of my relationship with Jesus were planted. These seeds were nurtured at Hope Community Church, where I listened to Stephen's voice, the strong strumming of his guitar, and watched his eyes, waiting for when they would close as his heart expanded outward, requiring only contact with the hearts of his listeners.

Now every morning when I wake up,
He's standing there, He holds my cup,
of sweet surrender, sweet surrender
to the will of the Lord."[2]

There is one as yet unmentioned experience that is appropriate to add here. One night, early in my relationship with Stephen, I had awakened from sleep to hear the sound of my name clearly and loudly spoken in the dark, terrifying me so much that I had looked around the small bedroom to see if somebody had entered. No one was there, and I didn't understand how I could have, without a doubt, heard a voice. As I gripped Stephen's arm, instantly waking him, he asked if something was wrong. So I told him...only to hear him say to give it to Jesus and watch as he rolled back and went to sleep. Feeling alone, yet having directions, I asked for Jesus and put out my hand, and that simple action began to calm me. Then in front of me and higher so that I was looking up, Jesus appeared in a vision of pale light, and I felt and knew His comfort.

Give Him your hand, He will guide you.
Give Him your mind, He will teach you.
Give Him your heart, you'll love so dearly.
Give him your life, He will remake you
In the image of God that lies within you ...[3]

Returning now to the chapter's opening quotation and reflecting on why I chose the Twenty-third Psalm and those particular lines from the King James Bible, I think that for many years this favored psalm in these few lines offered me the most comfort that I could find. I wasn't thinking about who "The Lord" was but instead about a shepherd taking me where there were green pastures and still waters—the distancing of a metaphor, yes, but of a scene of nature where I felt at ease.

CHAPTER 28

"Baba"

1997 – CONTINUING

God may be compared to the sandalwood.
It continually emits a sweet scent in all directions, though only those who take the
trouble to go near it have the benefit of its
charming fragrance.[1]

Meher Baba

While I have written personally of Meher Baba and my visits to His homes in America and India, this chapter begins with another's brief yet powerful explanation of how He became aware of His true state: "One day in May 1913, while studying at Deccan College in Poona, He (Merwan Irani known as Meher Baba) cycled past the venerable Muslim woman Hazrat Babajan, one of the five Perfect Masters of the time. She beckoned Him to her and kissed Him on the forehead, subsequently revealing to Him His true state as the Avatar, the total manifestation of God in human form."[2]

Meher Baba is referred to as the God-Man whose soul had come in previous incarnations and eras as Zoroaster, Ram, Krishna, Buddha, Jesus, Muhammed, and this time as Meher Baba. Distinct in this incarnation is that at age thirty-one He stopped talking and remained silent for over forty-three years, communicating by the use of an alphabet board, and later only through His own hand gestures. And yet, even from a silent place, He made it clear to his mandali that He was God:

> Baba told us to be natural with Him, yet He expected us always to hold Him in the highest respect. He said, "I come down to your level, but never bring me down to your level."...Throughout all, Baba's purity and divinity shone through His humanness, but sometimes when we became forgetful, He would have to say to us, "Remember, I am God."[3]

Baba is who He is to me now, but He came to me first known in prayer and song as "the Lord" and "Our Father," then as Jesus in visions, then as Meher Baba who I one day familiarly called "Baba." Retracing the steps of my spiritual journey to their beginning, I have reflected back to my twenties when I had a desire to have wisdom without knowing what that meant—nor did I understand the source of my desire. Yet this wanting continued. I associated it with a degree in philosophy, which I knew would have been impossible for me to achieve. It didn't occur to me that seeking wisdom could refer to a desire to know God, and as God was not a part of my life, eventually the desire was forgotten.

My first conscious step toward God had come in *A Course in Miracles*. In safety and comfort, supported by the group leaders and the others attending, at age forty-seven I had begun to let go of my fear of God. From the first night, my interest in what the reading was about and what I could learn only kept increasing. My religion was changing from one that took place in a church where my perception was that I listened to ideas to one of simply being in this group where I heard that all the words of the book could be summed up in one word—love.

My second step closer to God came during Stephen's and my time together, when in those years his deep connection with Jesus influenced me in a profound way. And it was during this same period that I had begun seeing visions that included Jesus. Then I met David Cousins in 1997, and through him heard of Meher Baba. I was fifty-four. Upon reflection, I see David as highly adept at what he had to do: turn me away from my familiar life toward a new direction of spirituality under the guidance of Meher Baba, who at times he referred to as "the big boss." David wisely and intuitively led me in a way in which I could remain within my area of comfort. The first time he mentioned Meher Baba, he made Him seem less significant than Sathya Sai Baba (who I'd met), telling me that Sathya Sai Baba was standing behind my right shoulder and Meher Baba behind my left. So I had merely noted Meher Baba's unfamiliar name. Another time, David spun a story that strengthened my relationship with Meher Baba but was only minimally noticeable to me at the time. In that story, I was the last of seven to get on a plane in which Sathya Sai Baba was the co-pilot, Mother Meera "the hostess with the mostest" and Meher Baba the pilot, who was telling me to hurry up. I focused on the group of seven, not on the pilot. My ability to take in David's stories unquestionably must have delighted him because he sensed well that had I been told the Avatar of the Age wanted me with Him in India, I would have bolted.

I've written about my first connections to Meher Baba that continued for seven months, from April through October 1997. During that time, David explained to me that I had one one foot on a magnetic highway and that once I put the other foot on there would be no going back. But my favorite thought of this time period is of the creativity of Meher Baba that ultimately had me laughing for His ways.

It was at that first August visit to Meher Center that I had begun to read about Meher Baba and felt confused by names that I didn't know and words with meanings that I didn't understand. But learning that His name was also "Compassionate Father" made Him seem like one I would want to know.

In the months after, whenever I heard an inner voice, I thought of Baba as a direct source—until I eventually understood that it was not always Him speaking but sometimes other guides within His awareness who I later learned to call agents. And perhaps it was because David had told me that my "contract" with Meher Baba had begun at the time of Jesus that I felt ineffable soul recognition of Him.

Thinking of those times when I had told others that I loved them, I could now understand that I hadn't known what love, the real kind, was. I could not give completely what I did not have completely, and I wanted to learn. Through the presence of Meher Baba I have been taught by means of daily life to think differently and so to speak and to act differently. When I suffered because change was difficult, He planted seeds of spiritual solutions in my thinking and feeling that grew into new understanding. Each time I remembered how I used to be, I appreciated that the suffering had been worth it.

My early visits to Meherabad had begun with a first pilgrimage for ten weeks from November 11, 1997 to January 1998. I had returned home with a stop in Singapore where my brother and his family were living on a two-year assignment—perfect timing for my altogether extraordinary journey. My second trip came that August. I had clearly felt drawn back, but could afford just one week. A year later, in the fall of 1999, I returned for five weeks. As the months of 2000 passed, I felt no urge to return, and in 2001 this was again true. It appeared that 2002 would be without hope until in August I heard by inner voice that I could do "no more counseling and no more fee charging." I returned in January 2003. Since then I have been in residence every year for nine to eleven months, and one time for eighteen months when my travel was restricted by an orthopedic doctor's orders.

It was in writing *Flower* that I finally put the missing piece of my interrupted pilgrimage into place. Meher Baba had been working with me in America through my ministerial training and counseling practice. Not only was His love and compassion increasing in me there, but He was also giving me a clientele for sharing this. When I did return to Meherabad, six years since first hearing His more complete name, He had become "Baba."

I want to include here one of my most memorable moments with Him, still remembered years later. On a day of a special event, there were hundreds of devotees surrounding Baba's shrine, the gem on the hilltop that spreads out down a gently sloped path to pilgrim housing. I was standing, waiting quietly, by a low metal fence that encloses the shrines of Baba, Mehera, His Beloved, Mani, His sister, and eight additional women mandali. Looking down from the north, I took in this large number of guests and then my breath caught. I saw Baba's spirit, as a vision, standing beside *every* pilgrim in view—hundreds of Babas, unmoving, looking straight ahead—until the full vision disappeared. I understood with freshness Baba's message that He is with everyone.

Although I wondered at first why I hadn't met Meher Baba when He was in His physical body, I finally accepted that my life was exactly right. Not only have I had the privilege to walk on the same ground where He walked but I have also sat alone in Samadhi, touched His chairs—gifts of immeasurable worth to me that I can now share with others as future pilgrims will no longer be able to enter the space, only look into it. And I have heard firsthand His remaining mandali tell their stories, their eyes radiating Baba's Love. Ultimately they ended all of anyone's questions with a single response:

"Just love Him."

CHAPTER 29

God-Given Gifts

1990–2004

I cannot expect you to understand all at once what I want you to know. It is for me to awaken you from time to time throughout the ages, sowing the seed in your limited minds, which must in due course and with proper heed and care on your part, germinate, flourish and bear the fruit of that True Knowledge which is inherently yours to gain.[1]

Meher Baba

From 1990 I'd had abilities of knowing in ways that I've heard referred to as psychic, occult, shamanic, dowsing, and Soul sensing. While I recognize that there are differences among these names, as topics I've felt little interest. What has been significant is seeing and understanding in new ways. In response to my having been questioned about a view I held, Dinesh Chibber, who I've found trustworthy over fifteen years as a spiritual teacher and as a close friend, said, "These are your God-given gifts." I valued his simple response. As for my abilities, they have come and gone according to what I needed to experience. I've held onto none when they ended.

What follows are situations that I found humorous, enjoyable, or enlightening and unusual in a world of the expected. All brought me information that I appreciated and learned from.

While I was moving into Jesse's farm, crows cawed each day, until pulled away from washing dishes or whatever else I was doing, I'd stand in the field staring up at them until they left. They brought a daily message of, "Hurry, hurry, hurry" that kept me working faster than I would have.

On a limerock road that I walked daily to the north past cow pastures and O'Leno State Park, my gaze often dropped to the road, searching. One day I saw three perfectly shaped petrified shells together, small, medium, and large, and delighted, as the road had never offered anything of such beauty, I tucked them in my shorts' pocket.

Hawks' shrill, metallic cries called me out of the house when they circled overhead, knowing to await a message, and within a few days a message would arrive. I once saw one I believed was intentionally waiting in a tree until I passed, watching as it then flew off. Then another time a hawk dove at my car door so swiftly that I moved my body away from the door as it swerved away with only inches to spare.

If fox, deer, armadillo, bat, turkey, rabbit, and snake crossed the road, the farm drive, the field, I searched for their meaning and found it concerned a part of my life that needed attention.

When David told me that blue roses meant help when needed, he energetically gave me three. After that, in a lucid dream, I saw ankle-deep blue roses completely covering a room's floor. Passing my sister's closet and glancing in, I saw that she had a dress of blue roses. When one of my Krishna clients came for counseling, she wore a dress with blue roses. At Christmas when we took out the farm collection of old ornaments, I found a small, clear globe with a tan and brown bird inside and on the bottom curve a blue rose.

In another lucid dream, angels as hundreds of dots of color were falling on twin beds where Megan and I slept. And in one dream I heard the names Helen Steiner Rice and Andrew Harvey[2] clearly spoken. Finding both of their writing, each had something to teach me for my counseling practice.

Before sleep, visions of faces from ancient cultures moved across my mind through different periods of time giving me new awareness of the vastness of eternity. I woke to a faint sun in my room one night. And on another, awoke calling, "Help, Allah."

For years clocks read 11:11 or 2:22 when I looked and addresses were 1111. On January 11, 1991, with Stephen, I attended an 11:11 event—"the number of masters who impacted humanity and shifted the vibrations of our earth throughout history"[3]—but I was spiritually young then and only remember a woman telling me my kundalini was rising.

At Meherabad, I found heart-shaped stones, and for years, green marbles before a trip back to America. Small black and white feathers appeared so often, I began a collection. When I found a single playing card I looked for a meaning in Robert L. Camp's *Love Cards*.[4] The final card of all that I found was the best—the King of Hearts, as Meher Baba was known.

Whereas the signs bolstered my well-being and made me aware

of a benevolent force present and guiding, I accepted that real truth lay within and that outside happenings were simply helpers on a journey of change.

CHAPTER 30

A Better Way

1999–2003

It does not require a large eye to see a large mountain. The reason is that, though the eye is small, the soul which sees through it is greater and vaster than all the things which it perceives. In fact, it is so great that it includes all objects, however large or numerous, within itself. For it is not so much that you are within the cosmos as that the cosmos is within you.[1]

Meher Baba

In June 1999, two days before Jesse was to leave for Meherabad, he asked if I would like to paint the outside of the farm to help with rent, and glad for a job I agreed. On my knees on the front porch, with a pail of cleaner, I softly cried as I pushed the scrub brush back and forth over the boards with cracks between them. I kept on crying, pushing the brush, glimpsing my lives as an Indian woman on her knees. I started repeating *ahimsa* (without harm), sending energy to Maheshi, the Gurumayi devotee I saw weekly at Hospice. Quietly I kept on crying for days, pushing the brush back and forth over other boards, fulfilling David's prediction that in two years I would experience all my Indian lives.

Because my life was so different from what I had known, every few months I would meet with Theresa Wesly at Unity of Gainesville, a woman who I highly respected for her role in the Church, to tell her my thoughts. She had also been to David's workshops and readings. She listened to what I found unbelievable, except for the reality that I was living it, until, satisfied, she raised her hand in a "stop" pose. "Do you feel stronger?" she would ask, and I always truthfully answered, "Yes." Once she added with a smile, "You're Baba's bride."

I found emotional growth harder than physical work. At the first reading, David had said that I had a strong mental grid but my emotional body was thin. I imagined three roads, mental, emotional, and physical, one above the other, with the mental on top. It was wide, but below it, the emotional was narrow due to my immaturity; and under that, the physical, where I waited, wasn't receiving information. To make that available, my emotional maturing was needed.

When David told me that my present situation would be harder than my previous one, I wondered how loving a man would be more difficult than losing one. But it was. (Then many years later an insight appeared. The previous love ties in my life, while expressing spiritual love, had been securely harmonized with romantic love. I was now in training to know more of God's love.) David further revealed that Jesse and I were "dredging up karma," meaning that we'd had past lives together that had not been completed, and he added that Meher Baba was "scrubbing off [our] spots," meaning getting rid of old views no longer purposeful or simply wrong. I held onto a simple Baba quote, as I kind of remembered it, that true spirituality is equanimity and poise in the face of everything. In these new ties, I was being shown what *was* love and what was *not* love—that to know real love came from within and had to do with me, and I could be wrong in how I perceived another. I guessed that it took Jesse's being very close to Baba to play this key role.

When I first said to Jesse, "I love you," and heard back, "I don't love you," I'd quickly answered, "That doesn't matter," followed by, "All that matters is how I feel." Surprised, I recognized a new and clear thought, but didn't know where it came from. I failed regularly and on occasion dramatically, but I had David's support—he had told me that I was meant to fail because in that event, I would look around for a better way.

Early on, when a casual comment to David one day caused him to see I was confused by different energies present in me, he gave me two descriptions, that of the camel and of the horse. The camel went slowly, worked through the third eye, and needed little water. The horse went fast, worked through the root chakra, and needed a lot of water. David then asked me to choose between them. I immediately chose the horse because of all the horse books I had read when I was ten. It was only later that I grasped its fuller meaning—it referred to Jesse and that my time with him would cause my fastest spiritual growth.

When I was told my eyes were open, while Jesse's were closed, I went to the *Discourses* and found a paragraph in which Meher Baba said He could do more when His lover's eyes were closed. Others could see who I was, but Jesse couldn't. Adjusting my sense of what was important to three things and letting go of the rest, I continued growing steadier in this new kind of love.

One day, standing at the sink washing dishes, I turned and told Jesse I had booked a ticket to India, as he already had his. I watched without moving, as his hurled coffee mug left a splattered brown stain on the ceiling before the crash of ceramic landed to my right. I turned back to the sink and continued washing, repeating silently what David had said. I might feel afraid, but I would always be safe as David had a constant cording of love (as energy) to me through this lifetime.

While my going to India required that I be able to get there without Jesse's help, another time when I told him of my trip, he said nothing, but later came to my room with a check for a thousand dollars. He told me to pay him back when I could, but to take care of other bills first. I saw him loving me as best as he could and, as Meher Baba's instrument, causing me to dive deeper into knowing my true self.

Whether Jesse and I were together, or one was in India for three months and one at the farm, I relied on Meher Baba and myself. The reliance came in many forms. In the fifth year, on one particular day, I had a helpful insight—an infrequent burst of anger directed at me caused me to look at my car keys as if I'd never seen them before. I chose the river, where from the bank, I watched water flowing by, reflecting the trees and wavering flights of birds. I felt inner stillness and calm. After this, when it seemed right to give him time alone, I took a book, learning that my inner voice or his phone call would tell me when to return. His explanation that he'd given the situation to Baba was the apology breathed between us not needing more words. Love in spite of differences kept growing as Baba's plan to rub our points of friction until we became frictionless kept working.

In January 2003, Jesse and I traveled separately to Meherabad, both having the intention of living there. I would be staying for five weeks this trip. It would be my "pilgrimage of tears." I remember few details for threads to weave a story of this time beyond seemingly unending tears. For the first twenty-six days, every time I went into Samadhi I began to cry, coming out with my face wet, wiping away tears that I didn't want seen. I thought they would never stop. During this visit, Jesse invited his friend Richard and me to take a car and driver to the temple of Perfect Master Sai Baba of Shirdi. As we reached the steps to get inside, I started to sob (not just cry) and this continued as we slowly moved in a long line, until Richard remembered that as Americans with passports we could go around to a shorter route up to the shrine, which we did. By then I had quieted. Throughout, Jesse had kindly ignored whatever I was going through, for which I was grateful. Facing the shrine I remember bowing down and placing my garland there, while men in robes lifted off the hundreds of garlands as fast as they kept building up and kept people moving.

Next that day we went to Secori to the ashram of Perfect Master Upasni Maharaj, who as one of the five Perfect Masters of the Age played an important role in Meher Baba's history. I seemed only to have been able to take in a few details, remembering now no more than stairs being pointed out where Mehera, at fourteen, had stood and had first seen Meher Baba walk by to meet with Upasni. When we entered the small darshan area, I sat to the right, in front of and apart from Jesse and Richard, not wanting to disturb them (or others), as again I was sobbing. Baba was releasing emotions I didn't understand.

Another time Jesse took me to Pune, to the shrine of the Muslim Perfect Master, Hazrat Babajan. It consisted of a small building with barely enough room to walk around her tomb and the large silver-painted base of a tree she had sat under. I first touched my forehead to the foot of the tomb bowing to her feet, then to her upper body bowing to her heart, where, holding still, I heard an inner voice speak, and assumed it was hers. Each time I returned with Jesse or on my own, I heard her speak to me. While Jesse took a beautiful garland, I could only take a small yellow rosebud from the flower stall to place over her heart, the difference seemingly representing his comfort and my shyness.

In February, mid-flight on my return to America, I heard an inner message that puzzled me: "You will return sooner than you think." The tiredness of travel changed to pleasure, but I wondered, how? I had one certificate of deposit for a thousand dollars that I was *not* supposed to touch. Then at the end of May, Baba spoke one word in a dream, "Come." I withdrew my certificate and reserved a ticket for three months later.

By August, Jesse and I both had tickets to India. Two days before Jesse was to leave, I woke at six and looking out the open sliding glass door, I saw him already at work and went into the yard. My jobs were to help prepare the garden and haul away the downed tree branches that he was pruning. The work progressed to a big live oak with branches hanging over the roof. To prune them, he was now standing on the tin roof, where he had to hold the shears straight up over his head. He had to be tired. As he pruned, I dropped the wood over the edge. Almost done, he moved to balance on a branch above the ground with his arms fully extended forward. In split-second lateness, as I heard the inner message "You are worth more than the branches," there was no time to tell him. He was falling head first, hands at his sides still holding the shears. Propelled six feet across the rippled tin roof, I reached out my hands and made contact with his body, breaking the fall. But the sudden impact of my weight on the roof corner with the pull of his body bent the corner, tipping me toward the ground.

Lying prone at his feet, in shock, traumatized by his motionless silence, and thinking that he was dead, I avoided looking at the odd angle of my left wrist to keep from fainting and screamed

"Jesse," then "Meher Baba," then his name again, wanting to see him move or hear his voice. Only later would I realize that his body had landed with his head directly toward the meditation studio at the edge of the woods and the photo of Meher Baba above the back doors.

Hearing him moan once, so knowing that he was alive, I got up, my body in pain from the fall but able to move, and holding my left arm out of view, I got to the phone—only to find the line dead. I didn't remember that I had unplugged it earlier. Getting my cell phone, I dialed 911 and was reporting the accident when that connection was lost because I was inside the house. Still hollering both names, I hunched toward my car and plugged the phone into the lighter. The cell phone was my first, and I didn't know what button to push to reconnect. I hit one, and in flooding emotion, heard the woman ask for a last name and directions.

As I rounded the corner to the backyard expecting to see him on the ground, I felt relief to see him slowly walking toward me. But my relief was short-lived. When I told him the medics were coming, instead of responding sensibly he asked, "Honey, why did you do that?" I had overpowered my pain to make the call, but now I sunk to the ground. I told him he had fallen off the roof and my wrist was broken, thinking this was a ridiculous conversation, until he began to reach for me, repeating he was fine. Then it struck me—he didn't remember. Raising my voice I said, "Don't touch me!" and pulled my arm back in panic over this new situation. At that moment I heard the siren of the emergency vehicle entering through the gate, and within moments four men surrounded us. One said he was Jesse's former sixth-grade student and, hearing his agitation, went to him to physically support and reassure him.

By the time we reached the hospital emergency room, Jesse's awareness had returned, but without details. He had no injuries, but his emotional pain for me was hard on him. We waited hours in a curtained cubicle. My composure held as I kept repeating that everything was for the best, and he gradually quieted. Strapped to the table, I thought of the war in Iraq. Then I thought of being in an American hospital without planes bombing it. I was safe, and eventually a doctor would come.

When staff members entered to check on me, I asked each to lean forward so I could see a face and then to give me a name, saying, "Thank you, I'm fine," to end concern. I couldn't turn my head. Walking and being x-rayed were painful, as I was barely able to move or hold the poses, and I felt faint. But I had Jesse and the radiologist holding me firmly, and they followed my directions when I needed to move or stand in order to drop my head to stop the whirling. Then by evening, we were back at the farm, driven in a hospital transport car.

Woman's wisdom told me I could manage on my own, even though Jesse offered to change his ticket. He needed to leave for India, and friends would help. Doing all he could for my comfort and rushing his packing, we left for the airport the following day with my friend driving.

When my daughter Beth asked why I hadn't thought before I moved, I couldn't answer her. I was moving—without thinking. Twelve years later I found the answer in Joseph Campbell's *The Hero's Journey,* a book filled with quotes by writers and philosophers who I had never read and probably would never read, but now benefiting me with right-sized exposure. Campbell gives an account of a paper, "The Foundations of Morality" by [Arthur] Schopenhauer, a nineteenth-century German philosopher, in which Schopenhauer asks, "How come, when the first law of nature is self-preservation, that is dispelled?"[2] As in my situation, why didn't I think of myself before moving to break Jesse's fall? The answer is that we act from a deeper impulse. Schopenhauer says, "You realize you and the other are *one.*"[3] We believe that we are separate, but this is an experience coming from the fields of time and space. My understanding is that time and space do not exist and reality is the present moment. Discovering that my action was actually determined by our spiritual realities, I drew in a big breath, and let it out in relief and in satisfaction. I'd done what was right; now I knew why. Beth's was a good question. Without it I would not then have felt a moment of enlightenment.

Two days after the fall, I faced the hand surgeon, who was carefully positioning my broken left wrist bones that the paramedics had splinted and told him I had a flight to India on August 28. "I'd like to be on it," I said. Then I smiled. In my short, yellow Indian dress with a Meher Baba button pinned on it, I was determined to show I could. I didn't know if he was answering me with his professional view or his heart, but he told me I would.

Not knowing what my medical opportunity would be in India, the doctor chose a sugar tong splint that I could remove rather than a cast. Lying on his table while the injected anesthesia and gel took effect, I focused on hope. When he told me he'd like to pull my hand and wrist apart so the bones could realign, I maintained my smile and reassured him I would make noise if needed, but to do what he had to. Breathing deeply I took Meher Baba's name aloud, but quietly, with the first pull, and to the doctor's amazement, remained silent. He directed the nurse to lock my elbow more firmly to the table and then pulled more strongly. This time I pushed my toes hard against the wall. Then it was over.

I listened to his directions to "follow my orders exactly," with a warning that if I didn't, the bones could become misaligned and might need to be broken and reset when I returned in February. That was a highly unpleasant thought. I knew what mattered though—I *was* going to be on the plane. When Baba's picture fell from where I had tucked it under my ace bandage, I asked if he had heard of Meher Baba. He said he had read Deepak Chopra. "Would you like this?" I looked at him, curious, and he answered yes.

As codeine dulled the ache, I packed for India. I did my short yoga practice mornings in tears, focusing on the quiet field and woods and friends for my daily comfort, then time beyond pain. One friend braided my long hair on doctor-appointment days, and the small-town librarian redid it. Figuring out how to move my standard shift one-handed, I quickly moved to independence until the last day, when my neighbor up the hill lifted my heavy suitcases. After driving to the automotive shop where the owner kept my car while I was away, I climbed into his high front cab and headed for the airport and my first stop—Atlanta.

EXPLORING

CHAPTER 31

The Hill in September

2003–2004

Mehera:...we four girls—Mani, myself, Naja, and small Khorshed, with Soona Masi and Valu—now stayed on the Hill.... We had only a bed, a trunk, and a little wooden stool each.... Our life was very strict...we only left our room to go to the kitchen for work, or to the bathroom, or when Baba occasionally took us for walks.[1]

Mehera

After breakfast was my favorite time to go up the hill where, before dawn, only watchmen opening Samadhi were allowed. The sun's early rays that pulled the gravelly ground out of dim light now fanned out, burnishing the finial above the white dome of the hilltop's gem.

To the right was Baba's cabin. Through its golden-yellow door open to similar walls, I saw fresh flowers, arranged before 6:30. Further to the right, aqua gates opened to the grassy rectangle of the upper compound, where neem and gulmohar trees shaded two old buildings—a water tank built by the British and a kitchen. At the end of 1933, the first Eastern women disciples lived here at Upper Meherabad. They were kept in seclusion away from the world for spiritual reasons. Baba had asked them to come (along with men He chose) for spiritual training in a community He was forming.

Now, the East Room of the water tank was for archival storage, the West Room was a museum, and the small, south-facing one where men disciples lived during the 1954 East-West Gathering, a library. The newer second floor was a large study hall behind the stem of a tower where Baba's rainbow flag fluttered in the breeze. When I was first learning directions and walking, and found my view of Samadhi blocked by the large, spiky cacti edging the dirt road, I would look for the flag to remember the right crossover path.

Going up the steep steps to the study hall, I unlocked the heavy padlock and walked to the back corner. As I closed the distance, my smile broke out, for what I was looking at was my favorite bronze statue of Baba, where His amazing eyes were smiling *at me*. Shutting mine and standing close, I balanced on my toes, touching my nose to His, and then pressed my forehead against the cool curve of His forehead. Each time, as in this visit, I saw a mental picture of Jesse's face, and heard him repeat, "Patience."

This September morning, as I hurried down the hill to my

room, I stopped to take in the beauty of the green fields that stretched as far across the valley as I could see, still except for the chatting of birds. Another warm morning had begun without a breeze. The low ground beside the path held recent monsoon rain. Because September was early in the pilgrim season, Meherabad wasn't full, but I had been here two weeks and felt the excitement of staying the six months that my tourist visa allowed.

I passed big trees with hanging roots, green umbrellas of protection from the sun's hourly-increasing intensity—the banyans, which once lined so many of India's roads, were gentle in appearance—friendly trees whose thick, outward curving branches opening from ample trunks at shoulder height reminded me of sitting on tree-branch seats as a girl.

When Baba chose this place, the hill and its farther skirt of land were bare. Now narrow paths went through tamarind and variegated tree orchards making shade canopies; wide paths crossed fields that rose at a slight angle or sloped more steeply to Lower Meherabad's flat land. Huge neem trees, watchful mothers, rose near Ahmednagar-Daund Road, where I crossed to the original Meher Pilgrim Center.

Softening the sere land in summer, invigorating it in monsoon rains, and partially hiding square, stone-block buildings with tile or tin roofs, yellow tacoma bushes stood willowy and tall, tangerine, rose, and pink bougainvillea branches spilled in curves, broad neems had delicate and tiny, fragrant white clusters, and glossy-leafed frangipani held handfuls of white stars. Red, white, or cranberry and faint-yellow hibiscus flowers with long, smooth petal-tongues opened at dawn to close by dusk, while myriad blue and purple blossoming vines meandered over wire fences.

Birds thrived in the semi-tropical climate—green parakeets, palest yellow-breasted oriental white-eyes, buff hoopoes with a startle effect of striped black and white wings, big birds with coppery wings bursting out from black bodies that perched, turning their heads to follow my movements, small birds that appeared black until white wing feathers flashed, and one infrequent and handsome onlooker whose splash of turquoise took a bite out of my incredulity. I watched them fly, hop, perch in the greenery and drink at water gutters and faucets that dripped with the regularity of clockwork.

Halfway across the world from where I once knew my only home, Meherabad entered my heart. The sun lit up the green or brown fields, the distant hills, and the shapes of the day, before it flamed into corals through shades of yellow to pastel pinks until finally fading to gray. And then darkness fell, with tiny human-lights, the moon, and the stars.

CHAPTER 32

A Message in Samadhi

2003

I am never silent. I speak eternally.
The voice that is heard deep within
the soul is My voice—the voice of
inspiration, of intuition, of guidance.
To those who are receptive to this voice,
I speak.[1]

Meher Baba

Samadhi is the small, airy shrine of Meher Baba, where a mural of muted colors covers the walls. A garden of heart-shaped garlands rises in a colorful pile on the altar cloths with Baba's simple words in gold leaf, on white marble: "I have come not to teach but to awaken." Only birdcalls, the movement of pilgrims coming in to bow down, or occasional, muted voices from the covered porch interrupt the silence.

Inside it is mainly blue. When I first thought about Baba and the people in the mural, I wondered why the artist had painted them in such a way that they didn't look real—until, one day, I felt longing for those strange faces and found a mural card to put in my room. My heart was opening to what my mind could not understand. Many years later, I would find an explanation when I learned more about Swiss artist Helen Dahm, who in 1938 had been invited by Baba to paint the walls. Helen's way of painting at that time was influenced by expressionism, a style that originated from a personal view of the world rather than a realistic one, in which distortion was used for an emotional effect. On that first visit of mine in 1997, while looking at the mural one day, I had intuitively known the comfort of Baba's arm wrapped around a pilgrim. I imagine now that Baba had envisioned this in choosing Helen.

In the morning, after the pilgrims left for breakfast, Samadhi was mostly empty. I would sit alone in the place I liked best, in front, on the right. With my left shoulder curved toward the wall, I turned my head toward the painting of Baba as a young man in a long, loose, white, dress-like sadra that fell below His knees. He sat in a field with a narrow dirt road winding away behind Him past a low tree and on to distant hills. As my gaze rested only on Him, I felt intimately alone, even if others were centimeters away. I talked to Him or gently corralled my wandering thoughts for inner as well as outer quiet.

This visit I found Baba's voice sterner, but only when I was in

Samadhi. Often I would hear one word, "Leave," and immediately I would. Each time, I would meet someone on the path back down who I would have missed had I remained. Most times it was Jesse. We'd share a few moments and, walking away, I would smile to have made the appointment on time.

One September morning, three weeks after arriving in Meherabad, I was sitting inside Samadhi when I heard, "Leave and begin writing." The brevity of Baba's words did not surprise me, but the direction to write brought a small, suppressed laugh. Two weeks before, I had emphatically told my friend Rose that I was not going to write about my spiritual experiences and dredge up the past. It had been difficult enough to live. Immediately kneeling before the shine and only glancing at the painting, I touched my forehead to the altar cloths and left the tuber rose-sweet air. As I walked to my room, I asked for Baba's help in remembering what was to be retold as I had taken no notes the past seven years, having needed all my strength simply to endure.

CHAPTER 33

My Room

2003–2004
this is your home
Adi Dubash

Sitting on sturdy, blue and white block-printed cotton Indian sheets, with a café au lait and burgundy bolster sewn with small mirrors firm at my back, I looked through the tall, wide window and open door into the courtyard of the Pilgrim Center, a brick residence softened by flowering frangipani trees. A palm with twelve-foot fronds, the remaining half of an old frangipani tree, and, arching over the roof, a vine thick as a strong leg made small caves of shadows. Above me the ceiling fan turned, barely audible, hanging from the tan matting-and-beam roof.

To make my bed a home in the room I shared with three others, I had put a row of blue and white plastic baskets underneath it, along the edge that I swung my feet over, to hold things for the bathroom, household and office needs, shoes, and books. Three soft, natural cotton bags full of hats, a black umbrella with silver lining, folded Khadi cotton and Kashmiri wool scarves, and a thermos bag with cinnamon sticks drooped by their handles on the corners of the metal, mosquito-net frame.

In the closet, more bags separated sweaters from tee shirts, pajamas, and under-things on shelves beside a pole with Punjabi dresses—the three-piece dress, scarf, and pants whose double width waist ties with a drawstring. I kept an old, gray-green L. L. Bean jacket hanging near my pillow so that getting out of bed at night I could easily reach my friend-for-warmth. Zipping in the fuzzy, blue lining reminded me of the southern coast of Maine, where I'd bought it, and the cold, deep blue of the Atlantic Ocean that I missed.

When my room assignment was in Hostel D, at Lower Meherabad, in a row of eight iron cots, each with a small alcove and a closet, I read and wrote, taking a warm drink to my bed that was home. Air flowed through brick latticework under a high roof. In cold weather, at night I draped blankets over the frame and wore a sweater and scarf, with my hat pulled down to my eyes, to allow me to quickly cross the dirt road to the toilet-room, where I had stars for a roof. In hot weather, I chose a bed under a fan, and hoped the woman next to me liked a rush of air, too.

This morning I had moved back from the Dharamsala, then Hostel D, because I had lived the longest at the Pilgrim Center and was the first reassigned when it was full. The Dharamsala is a smaller residence in an old building with fewer beds situated on each wall and a corner wash up and toilet room. I was delighted to be there as the larger Hostel D is housing for Indian women who noisily begin their day at three a.m., and a dirt road has to be crossed to a large bathing and toilet room. But Hostel D also had a benefit: each night I heard *bhajans*, devotional songs, sung at nine on the veranda after dinner where, a few feet away, I fell asleep to soft, sweet soprano voices filling the night with the Eastern raga.

On my first day at the Dharamsala, as I had entered, about to turn to look for an empty bed, I stood unmoving instead, my eyes on a photo I'd never seen before, positioned high on the far wall, of a white horse looking directly out. Suddenly I remembered thumbing through magazines at my parents' home looking for pictures for writing exercises and finding a face of a white horse on a cover.

My history with horses seemed natural for a girl, but my experiences as a mother at forty-nine had gone unexplained—riding my dusty-golden mare in inner seeing, keeping the plastic Appaloosa on my bedside table and the photo of the white horse on my desk—yet all had brought pleasure, important comfort, and my trusting acceptance.

The photo of the white horse remained on my shelf for four years until Stephen and I moved to Florida. Having spent weeks of late nights going through writing notebooks and materials, I couldn't see taking the photo of the white horse from a nine-room house with an attic and basement to a six-room apartment I hadn't seen. It wasn't practical, yet I felt sad. Now I wish that

I'd followed my feelings, but instead I put the photo into a big, plastic bag and said my good-byes.

Twelve years later, after I had discovered the painting of the white horse at the Dharamsala, I was amazed to read what Mehera had said to Babajan:

> I said to Babajan, "I want a horse."
> "Yes, He will be very beautiful,
> all the world will love Him."[1]

I wondered if my white horse, like Mehera's, had been Meher Baba. (Later Mehera actually did have a white horse that Baba gave her, which she rode.) Every morning of those early years, I had paused between my bedroom and the kitchen, in the east light of the big window to gaze at the white horse, wordlessly loving it. If Meher Baba was introducing Himself in this way, unsuspecting, I had fallen for love.

CHAPTER 34

Write Deeper   •

2004

Writing as a spiritual practice is a hero's journey, a
journey that in some way every human being must
make. Each of us has his or her own bag of tricks,
a personal mythology made up of certain moments
that we carry with us, consciously and unconsciously,
understood or not at all understood.[1]

Pat Schneider

Having left Samadhi and walked rapidly down the hill, I'd come straight to my room. Sitting cross-legged on the blue and white bed sheet, I opened my computer to a blank page, wondering how I would do this as my left wrist was still splinted. Immediately I remembered Baba pointing with one finger to his alphabet board. I waited—and finally a thought came. With one finger I typed "The Hayloft" and began. For six weeks, I held my hand upright, or when sleeping, rested it on a pillow. When the codeine prescription ended, it still hurt badly. Freed of the splint, on the first morning, I went to Samadhi and laid my hurting arm on the stone, putting my good arm on top and my head on both. The smooth coolness penetrated, lessening my pain, and I came each day for Baba's therapy. Until December, when I could use two hands, my stories would be written in this one-finger way. Other stories appeared, bringing with them new awareness of their early spiritual significance. I felt excited and knew Baba as the source of my remembering.

Not finding enough time to write by day, I draped a blanket over my bed frame, until the escaping light woke my roommate. Then I moved to the large, lighted toilet room and sat next to laundry that was soaking in basins on the wooden bench. I dove into the past—obsessed with remembering. Jesse, upon discovering this, had me sit down with him for a talk, and with a kind, but unwavering gaze, pointed out that by withdrawing from visiting the mandali, I was missing a valuable opportunity. From then on, I better controlled my day and night schedules.

When I asked several women if they'd be willing to read my writing, Cynthia was in the group that accepted, and I gave her my first chapters. Cynthia was from a town in Western Massachusetts closer to Vermont than where I'd lived, but it, too, was a turn off I-91 North. When we talked, I imagined driving by fields shaped by the intermittent Connecticut River, then by the distant, protective Berkshire Hills lit by early eggshell skies, or purple, red, and orange floes of sunsets topped with circling hawks. We met during this, my first six-months' pilgrimage to Meherabad, and my love for that remembered drive fused to our shared interests, created a friendship that would last, and in time turn toward my writing.

Now, when I knocked on her door at eight o'clock for dinner, she turned from her desk, and framed against the tall, dark window by warm light, said she wanted to finish. The next day, she told me she liked the writing and wanted to read more when I wrote it (as had several other women), but Cynthia was the only one who handed me notes. The folded eight-and-a-half by eleven-inch paper had writing down one side and across the bottom corner. She wasn't trained, she added, but said she had a natural ability to edit. I bypassed her punctuation notes and went to the comments where her wanting to know more told her that I needed to "write deeper." My stomach felt empty. I knew I was not telling enough and feared telling more. What I didn't know then was that to write deeper, I needed to mature emotionally to first find what was missing *in me*.

The second sign that my writing was to be of a different nature came in January, on the blue bus to Meherazad. I was listening to an interesting conversation, coming from the seat behind me where a friend sat with a young man who I didn't know, about Prof. Amiya Kumar Hazra, a noted disciple and follower of Meher Baba. I turned to be introduced. The woman who was my seatmate had also been listening, and now we both met Titu, the grandson of Prof. Hazra. My seatmate had just read Prof. Hazra's book, *The Memoirs of a Zetetic: My Life with Meher Baba*[2] in a day. My friend was still reading it, and based on their enthusiasm, I knew I had to read it too. Titu invited us to his grandfather's home, a fourteen-hour train ride to Jabalpur. We had heard of others who had visited, discovering the professor's deep love for Meher Baba and his welcoming invitation for pilgrims to stay.

Deciding to go with Titu, we turned our discussion to train tickets.

That afternoon, upon returning to my room, I pushed open the screen door with its closing brush whisper, and heard my inner voice say to simply buy the book and not make the trip; I felt disappointed, but relieved. The lengthy train hours without the kind of food I needed would have lowered my energy. Overtired, I would not keep up my strength, and I did not want to become a difficulty for others. (A good deal of years later I did meet Prof. Hazra, finding that his inner light truly was his demeanor.) I finished a quarter of the book before stopping, having to discipline myself to return to my own writing. What riveted me were the challenges Prof. Hazra repeatedly gave Meher Baba to quell his doubt that Meher Baba was God and the signs that Baba gave him. I was reading experiences similar to mine, except that I had not thought to ask for anything in particular. Amiya Kumar Hazra's journey gave me new awareness of Baba as unfathomable, even to those who knew Him earlier.

As I continued reading, it became clear that even though I barely knew Titu, I was to ask him if he would read "The Hayloft." The next day he agreed. At the screen door, my inner voice this time said, "Give him all of it." Immediately I knew I wanted to, but paused, considering that the act of handing my writing to someone not trained to respond with only encouraging comments and no criticisms at this early writing stage as I had been trained to do could be a risk. Hearing the instruction a second time, I took him thirteen chapters, and told him my concern.

When I went to pick up the pages, he had read three chapters and wanted to finish the rest in the hour before the bus left for the train to Jabalpur.

"Done," he'd said, smiling, when I returned. "Your writing is wonderful. You don't need to visit my grandfather. But may I say one thing?"

"Yes."

"I can feel Baba through all of this, but you must write about 'what happened with you and Baba,' as the readers will need to know." Speaking quietly, his eyes watched to see if I was upset. Relieved and elated, I let go of my fear of taking no notes, and, instead, heard Baba affirming my first efforts through both Cynthia and Titu, who had each brought messages from Baba that I had to respond to. Going back to my room I typed "Message in Samadhi."

Then, a month later, on a February night, my computer stopped working. Impatient after an hour's effort, I asked, "Am I supposed to stop writing?" and the answer came back "Yes." What Meher Baba started and sustained, He now stopped. Accepting this, I lay down and closed my eyes.

CHAPTER 35

Love Alone Prevails

2004

Love can be blind, selfish,
greedy, ignorant but love
with understanding can be
none of these.[1]

Meher Baba

Prior to my leaving India in April 2004, two months after my writing had stopped, Jesse told me I could no longer stay at the farm. I'd told him I would face that when I arrived. At the field gate, I tried the key. The padlock had been changed, but I could fit between the end of the gate and the woods. It was eleven at night and raining, and I'd been traveling over forty hours. Pragmatically, I carried my suitcases to the farm on my head, found candles and lit them, checked the outdoor gas tank to find it was unlocked, and listened as the stove burners lit...with a hiss. For two weeks, buying water and working by daylight, I gave away or sold most of what I owned and made a plan. I had two women friends in the Blue Ridge Mountains who might let me stay a number of weeks...and found that they would.

The day before I was to leave, the phone rang. Unusual, I thought. It was Jesse calling from India to ask why I was still there. I told him I was leaving, only to learn that the purpose of his call was to tell me where the gate key was. I told him my car was already loaded and smiled, hanging up.

The next day, in my '98, red, two-door Cavalier full of what mattered in my life, leaving only my bed and a few basics, I drove through the farm gate, saying, "I will only be grateful for living here."

Within minutes, I realized that I was on an adventure that grew in excitement as I closed the distance to western North Carolina. Reaching the mountains, feeling pleased, I figured out that Baba, in his reverse way of teaching, was giving me a beautiful vacation. Not fully comfortable in my freedom, each day I relaxed more deeply in my close friendships and the enclosing protection of the Blue Ridge Mountains that actually *were* blue. Hiking up dirt trails, I stopped by foamy waterfalls, admiring them, wondering how I could be so fortunate. I drove up the spiral road of Mt. Pisgah and back, looking at irregular patches of sun among differing shades of green and trees, thin, fat, tall, short, healthy, askew—all quiet but for my engine.

I accompanied a friend one night to a restaurant where the group from a workshop with David Cousins was eating. I hadn't had readings with David for over four years and my final workshop with him had been two years earlier. Seeing him was a surprise, as I hadn't known about this workshop. Our meeting turned out to be helpful, as always. When the meal had ended, people who lingered kept asking me to move closer to talk to them, until I found myself opposite David at the table. I took the opportunity to tell him that I had no home and no job—a pivotal moment in my relationship with David. For ten minutes, he assumed his former role, explaining to me that I was to read his poetry (which I did later that evening) and know that I had three options for where to live. By morning I would know the answer. Of Asheville, North Carolina, Australia, and the farm, I hoped I would return to the farm.

However, longing for more guidance, I left for Meher Center. Arriving tired from the long drive I promptly fell asleep, waking at three in the morning to walk with my flashlight to the Lagoon Cabin. There, where Baba had brought me guidance over the past seven years, I knelt in deep relief in the soft glow of the small lamp. I asked Him what to do. He answered.

The next day, following an invitation for prayer and breakfast at a nearby home, I found myself sitting on the floor by the woman whose home it was, listening to her talk with another woman and becoming increasingly interested in what the second woman was saying about her work with her husband, who was also present. Crossing the room to talk with him, as I spoke, I realized that I was slowly revealing more about myself to him than he was revealing about himself to me. I didn't know that he was a psychiatrist, adept at listening and evoking more than casual conversation. When he told me he thought I would benefit from meeting a particular woman, I went to the phone and dialed Arlene Stearns, but got no answer. The next day I reached her and with directions to her home, went to visit. I later learned that the couple at whose home we were did not regularly open their home for prayer, the wife and husband did not usually go, and that this woman who had invited me to her home rarely saw people.

I sat on Arlene's sofa on the sunny, glassed-in porch in a country neighborhood, facing trees and blue sky, becoming aware that she talked not only about Meher Baba, but about what I understood as New Age information. Unlike me, Arlene spoke mainly with Meher Baba's words. Growing more and more agitated, I felt tears wet my cheeks, dripping from my chin onto my hands.

On my earliest visits to Meherabad, some had frowned when I spoke of my occult experiences, and being new, I interpreted that as meaning that *I* was frowned upon, resulting in my feeling isolated. I found some small comfort with those who listened, without judgment, and referred to Meher Baba bringing me there, but too often I would withhold my story, as it was all I knew and trusted. The information that I had worked to limit in any talks with Baba lovers, Arlene integrated into her conversation with His words. My self-protective layer thawed, and the tightness in my muscles loosened. I gradually slumped forward until my shoulders rounded in limp posture and relief saturated my entire body.

My pain poured out in the utter safety she offered. A small thought gathered momentum until, with my voice like a child who realizes that she is secure, I said, "I think I'm here to learn to talk more like you, using Baba's language." Fear that I might have to change myself, or leave Baba, evaporated. Her smile, like the sun on my lap, warmed my now quiet body. She was a friend in a way no other had been. Driving away, I knew I'd found what I'd come for. Meher Baba had shown me the meaning of a book I'd read about Him—*Love Alone Prevails.*[2]

After seeing Arlene, and soon before I was to leave, I found and bought the book, *The Silent Teachings of Meher Baba*, which also affirmed that my journey to Baba had been exactly what it was supposed to be, and when it had been time for me to change, Baba had made that happen.

Taking in the view of the ocean and stopping for a moment to put a pot of orange marigolds on the Lagoon Cabin steps, I then left. Over the next week, I traveled to California and had a last visit with Stephen's daughters. When, a year later, they told me that they were fine and that it was time to end our relationship, I knew that I would go on loving them, and be in touch from time to time, but they were right. In this completion, Baba was opening up my life.

I stayed a final week in Gainesville with a young woman preparing for a lessened, yet still arduous, two-year correctional sentence. On her first visit for pastoral counseling, I recognized every holy woman I knew pass across her face. At her home, with her boyfriend, her dog, and cat, I welcomed the hoped-for-call from Jesse to return to the farm.

CHALLENGING

CHAPTER 36

Jesse and David

1997–2004

The ego-life has a beginning and an end:
the Truth which I bring is beginningless
and endless. In order to inherit that Truth
you need the courage to jump across the
abyss of duality.[1]

Meher Baba

In the preface I wrote that facing an abyss at fifty-four and trusting my spiritual teacher, I made a leap of faith toward real love. David had established himself as safe to work with at our first meeting, even though he spoke of challenges faced and those to come. I'd had many past lives that were "horrid and grotty" but gave me a big bank of information. I had to cross a river with piranha, but guides were positioned upstream and downstream so I would be safe. My present life would be "blood, sweat, and tears," and I would need to be over 90% successful at passing the given tests.

I have no explanation for why I was able to calmly listen to him, aware of metaphor, unless in a past life I had been prepared and was standing on a foundation unobtrusively supporting me. When David told me I was crossing over an "abyss" with my "lighter twin in contest with my darker twin," in my words I had to overcome any doubt and face the unknown with willingness, courage, and action propelled by faith in Meher Baba. On the side of the abyss where I stood was romantic love, where I looked for what I could gain. On the opposite side was real love, where I looked for what I could give. (I later learned that duality with Meher Baba meant that to see gender as a reason of difference misses the truth of oneness.)[2]

That first January of 1997, David had spoken of "a very fast lightworker who had me in his little black book." He gave no name, and I didn't ask. Reading of accomplishment versus potentiality, it was the latter within me that freed me to go into the unknown with a map of mostly metaphors and a certain amount of direct information from a man I didn't know but with whom I'd felt immediate trust and unrealized soul recognition.

In April I had a call from the lightworker that David had mentioned but didn't recognize him; neither did I when we met in May. Finally, at some point that summer, I put together the April phone call and the May visit, and knew David's reference was to

Jesse. That October, as I was preparing for my first trip to Mehe-rabad, I moved onto Jesse's farm, by his agreeing from India that I could, and met with David again. I told him that I felt I'd had many lives with Jesse. "Oh, feels like an old shoe, eh?" David had said with his eyes twinkling.

Jesse wanted nothing to do with David, wanted me not to talk about him or see him, which made it difficult, as I wanted to talk. But Jesse expressed himself strongly every time I forgot (and I did), and he just wouldn't allow it. Jesse had personal reasons. And so, I had to validate my journey from within.

What David told me was that Jesse was on one side of me and he was on the other side and together they were pushing against me until my male and female energies were "nicely 'squoshed' to-gether." I knew of no visible communication between them yet felt that on some plane, they were meeting in weekly strategy ses-sions for my spiritual growth. Each was my teacher in different roles. I resolved not to try to figure them out because it would do no good, and instead concentrated on my leap beyond love with dependency to love with God.

David had explained his presence in my life as needing to find the daughter I'd been (I was one of his children) in Roman times. My final workshop with him was on February 20, 2002, which written as an Indian date is 20 02 2002. It was the last of sev-en extended weekends spread over seven years, and by its unique combination of numbers, a clear sign of its import.

When he told me (at that workshop) that he was my "door-way to Samadhi—and the bouncer at the door," initially I thought of him as the doorway, and Jesse the bouncer (David was never direct with his referrals about Jesse). Finally I decided it didn't matter; both roles were necessary. Consequently, I was fully unprepared for David's December email in 2004. Its sug-ary wording inviting me to be on his team hit me hard—twice. First was my reputation (David teased me in front of workshop participants) as the only woman who refused to hug him. So I found his sugary words offending—as he intended. His role was not only to bring me to Baba but to be sure I stayed; this was my final test. Second, I had desired to be on his team since my early contact with him. Mentally, I knew I was Baba's alone, and I understood there was, in fact, no choice. But my reaction went from stunned awareness to a tsunami of sobs and gasping. Years later when editing this book, with deeper emotional balance, I saw the reality. Had I accepted David's offer to join *his* team, he would have become the "bouncer at the doorway to Samadhi."

Two people helped me through this time period: Jesse, who continued his vociferous insistence that I only needed Meher Baba, and Arnavaz, a mandali, who had taught me when I first arrived in Meherabad that my story didn't matter, only that I loved Baba. Six years later, I remembered how sympathetic her help had been, and made an impromptu visit. She watched as my face flooded with tears, again since the email had arrived, and in a ragged voice I told her of the tearing apart I felt. Although in her eighties, and having difficulty with one leg, she stood and in an unexpected move walked slowly to her table for a box of tissues to give me, reversing my usual role as I sat, helpless to move. The significance registered. With me quiet, she then spoke kindly of this man, saying only that once I came to Baba, I had no need for another, even a perfect master. My heart heard. That afternoon I sent an email of appreciation and finality to David.

A week later, an insight reduced me to laughter until I was almost crying—gratefully—from laughter and not from loss. I remembered that first year I'd met David and wanting so much to be on his team that I'd asked if I would. He'd said there would be two of us making the decision. I didn't know the opportunity would not be offered for another six years, or that the other one making the decision would be Jesse. My answer had been known as soon as I asked. That morning on the porch with Arnavaz had significance beyond her actual words. As her large, brown eyes unwaveringly held mine, I had heard another message within.

Child,

> I have taken you on my lap and comforted you,
> as you deserve, and now you are fine.

CHAPTER 37

On My Own

2004

Indian roads are also the scene of what the
western world confines to the farm, pasture
or playground: bullock carts, cyclists, troops
of pedestrians and beggars, herds of goats
and sheep, stray cows.[1]

Rano Galey

During the first three years I came to Meherabad, I lived in Trust housing and ate in the dining room, then after three years of not returning, by 2004, and the second six-month visit, I moved into my first two-room home. Deciding early that I wanted to take care of myself rather than have a bazaar shopper meant my learning my way around part of it with its thousand stalls in a town named Ahmednagar that had been the sixteenth-century seat of a powerful Muslim kingdom.

I rode in a rickshaw for the twenty-minute ride to town, tying a bandana over my nose at a turn-around on its outskirts when the smell of petrol became strong. Fields and small homes turned into a motorcycle business, stands for fruit, dishes, and rugs, and, closer to town, tire sales. A little way back, fenced behind road congestion, the quieter demeanor of the Ahmednagar College buildings faced a large, shady area of trees that softened the reflected metal of a tightly packed sea of bicycles.

As this was a festival day, a narrow river of white and yellow chrysanthemums wound along a roadside interrupted by sellers seated on cloth, while at standing-height, garlands of bright blossoms tied with dark-green leaves hung from the horizontal poles of wooden carts.

First asking inside the bank one floor up for the exchange rate, I withdrew rupees from the ATM, dropped off a film two doors away, and then down one flight from street level checked my email at a cyber café.

From the side of the main street, I looked in one direction and, with fast decisions, crossed halfway between cars, trucks, motorcycles, bicycles, bullock carts, hand-pushed carts with bicycle wheels that didn't observe traffic lanes, and cows lying or standing. I was headed for a restaurant whose young owner Meherabad people liked. Facing the other direction, I took the final steps. Lunch was plain rice, dal, and veg, eaten while watching Indians tear off small pieces of roti bread to scoop up spicy sauces and fried vegetables, or with a spoon dip into the restaurant's special-ty—a dish of fresh tropical fruit ice cream.

My next stop was the Meher Baba Trust Office on the main Station Road. From there I walked straight back two blocks, crossing an intersection where, on the far side, a watch store with a sign in English was my first landmark. Next was the rice district, so jammed some days that I had to turn sideways to squeeze by intricately painted red, blue, and yellow rice transport trucks. Where the road ended, I turned left at a row of both fresh and faded pastel buildings. Following a short curve, I arrived at the gold bazaar, then passed the big vegetable market and hardware bazaar to emerge at a long, narrow alley that led to a divided lane of clothing shops, and at the end, my destination—MG Road that memorialized Mahatma Gandhi. Eventually I stopped having to think so intensely about directions and moved about without concern.

Today, I had brought a blue sapphire necklace that I wanted shortened. I found a woman with jewelry tools, seated on the ground under an umbrella who charged less than a dollar and put the small now unneeded gems into an intricately folded newspaper packet.

Next I needed dog collars for a friend, and used English, hand gestures, and facial expressions until a "shoe wala" (seller) understood, helped by onlookers who added their interpretations in Marathi.

At first, I struggled with vendors who asked did I want this or that, until I realized they weren't going to stop. I learned to say No in Marathi and to look them in the eyes until we both smiled, and they gave up.

I bought a half-kilo of chiku fruits, small, round, and fuzzy, with big, shiny, black seeds; two football-size green papayas, smooth and red inside; and a coconut with the top cut off, so that as I drank, milk dripped off my chin.

Indoors at the large, dim market, with vegetables on one end, and cows near open, smelly eastern toilets on the other, I soon knew which sellers had the best carrots, beets, okra and spinach, pumpkin and ginger that day, and went to those, leaving with bulging plastic bags.

Walking by the bangle shops, I didn't turn toward the men asking me, "Yes, Madame, what would you like?" Instead, I headed for shops with stainless-steel pressure cookers, storage tins, buckets, and baskets, and then the grocery store, where I bought ghee, basmati rice, and sunflower oil, dish soap, and sticks and seeds of spices.

Speakers of Hindi, Marathi, and English, and the crooning of animal tenders surrounded me. Drivers sounded horns and bells. Goats and cows foraged or watched from folded legs. Dogs with drooping teats slept or prowled. On narrow streets with no sidewalks, I moved by business owners looking out open doors at a flow of motorcycles, bikes, cars, and rickshaws, with shoppers, groups of school children in uniforms and rubber sandals, and beggars without hands or a leg sitting on the ground or on low, push carts—all who might briefly look as I mingled among them.

When done, I left the chaos, body tensed during the bumping ride, until reaching the fields, I relaxed, feeling safe closer to home; then, with a deep breath of accomplishment, got out at quiet, tree-populated Lower Meherabad.

CHAPTER 38

West and East

2007

A Questioner: Is this path-finding more difficult in the
West than in the East?

Meher Baba: No. It is a different outlook, because
in the East as in the West there are in-
tellectual giants. Also in both there are
good hearts. And in the teachings of
great men, both East and West, there
is love; only the name and method are
differently expressed.[1]

From notes at the farm, January 2007: So quiet, so still inside the farm, I can hear the hum of the universe within me. Outside, hanging laundry, insects have the microphone. Two frogs sat with me on the patio as night deepened beyond the curves of daylily leaves. He came first then she emerged from under my chair. She leaped into the pond of grass first. He followed. And I went in to bed.

Leaving the sanctuary of the farm I returned to Meherabad.

One morning when I was in the Upper Compound working on a museum plaque at my assigned Trust job of cleaning brass plaques, with a large collection of implements surrounding me, a woman I was friendly with walked up. She stopped. I was kneeling on the ground. Looking up I reminded her that I'd like to see her new home, as I'd been invited. "But I'm leaving for England in two hours. Can you come now?" Within minutes all of my items were in her car as she drove us off the hill, turning onto a narrow, poorly maintained road between two towns then down her dirt lane to the back of a field.

Standing outside her large compound, seeing the surrounding land empty of all but the small, low-built home of the farmer family who had owned the land before its sale, I knew this was to be my home. Jesse joined us, then the realtor. I told him I'd like to buy a plot. I chose an elongated square, at a distance from my friend. It equaled one-eighth of an acre, was two kilometers from the hill, and on a corner where I could have an east-facing kitchen with a long field as my view. Later I found a large pointer crystal in the rough grass of my plot without a geological reason to be there. I took it as a confirmation of my decision.

To celebrate my excitement and Jesse's for me, he suggested that we go to the Valley of the Saints, a long drive to the spiritually historical rock-cut temples of Ellora Caves. While in the Jain Cave, I approached a large statue of a lion with its head up, facing forward and legs folded under. When near enough to touch, in an unexpected movement I was clasping my arms around its neck and kneeling, leaning on its body as I wept. Once I turned to see if I was upsetting Jesse, but he only quietly glanced my way, appearing to understand that I was releasing a previous life. Then suddenly quiet and still, I was fine.

CHAPTER 39

My Scooter

2009

Remember when you stumble,
My hand is extended to lift you
up.[1]

Meher Baba

It was the week of my sixty-sixth birthday when I bought an electric scooter to conserve on petrol for my car and immediately recognized that I didn't like speed—a definite drawback. Not wanting to give up, I continued practicing at a speed as slow as I could go. One day, approaching the open gate to my compound from an, as yet, untried angle, the front wheel tilted on the rail set in cement, and scared, I slowed down—a wrong move. The scooter tipped, jammed my knee against the rail, and I, although unaware, had seriously broken a bone. Able to pull my leg out from under the scooter, I could move no further without excruciating pain. My calls for help then Meher Baba brought unmet neighbors to my aid, but in a group now gathered, the efforts of three men to lift me intensified the pain, and I kept repeating Stop!

With the ambulance waiting, the medical staff that had arrived strapped me onto a stretcher and once inside, my neighbor's wife (Kathleen I now learned) climbed in with me, beginning to sing as we started. Her Hawaiian songs both reassured and diverted me from thinking about more than gripping a rail to lift myself up at every bump as I inwardly repeated that something good was going to come from this.

Seventeen days later, in summer's hot, dry, dust-blowing days, with most foreigners gone, I faced three months of home confinement, except for x-rays. So calling this my adventure and seated on my computer chair, I pushed around my apartment, started a pamphlet project on my computer and leaning on the counter, standing on my good foot, learned I could both cook and wash dishes on one foot.

Then Baba stepped in. My new neighbors, artists I learned, decided to visit with their paintings, turning my home into a museum with tour guides. As I know little about art, I asked if each would explain his and her work, Billy first then Kathleen. As days passed, I began hoping to see a painting with water, which I missed very much living in this semi-desert. Then one day Kathleen came far enough through the door for me to see a white bear, swimming in foam-rippled aqua water, and my hope rose! The painting was huge, metaphoric, and I knew, mine.

One day, seeking an alternative to boredom by looking out the triple-wide window to the hilltop, I felt drawn to hold up my hand toward the window so that my palm and fingers were a gentle curve facing the glass. As I did, I saw a vision of a white rose appear with its petals slightly lifted from my palm, then smoothly leave and fly in a straight line to the hilltop and Samadhi. Every day now, for a period, I would hold up my palm, but changing my thought to a different individual each time, a difference in the size of a rose or in the number of roses I saw as symbolic of that person's spirituality.

As my recovery was steady but slow, keeping me confined, I began to think of people permanently on crutches, or in wheelchairs, or hand-pedaling three-wheel bikes, and if without legs, riding on a wagon inches above the ground that they pushed by their hands—people I had passed and given a mere glance to, admiring their courage but without feeling compassion for them. This was the most restrictive period of time I had ever known, and the experience changed me. I would walk again, but Baba was training me in new understanding of those who would not, awakening greater compassion.

On July 4th, although it was with a duck's waddle, I walked up to Samadhi after five months. When my retired friend the professor asked if I was running, of course he knew I wasn't, but I liked his humorous strategy. I told him that I was dancing to Tony Bennett's "Steppin' Out With My Baby"—holding onto the kitchen counter.

CHAPTER 40

Trials

REFLECTIONS: MY 70S

God cannot be explained, He cannot be argued
about, He cannot be theorized, nor can he be
discussed and understood. God can only be
lived.[1]

Meher Baba

Growing up in New England, in cold, snowy Januaries, I watched my mother cut long branches of forsythia with small bulges the thumb could feel, then stand them in tepid water in a pitcher once her mother's. Within days, buds bound by freezing temperatures burst into summer's yellow eyes.

My father and Jesse, I could say, forced me by a different, stronger method to turn to spirituality. In retrospect, they were the hardest on me of anyone in my life. They confronted, challenged, denied who I was, and gave their views as right. But they were the ones most responsible for my strengthening in determination to know myself and go beyond the limitations I had lived with. I came to recognize that their love was from the soul, as well as worldly, and it was directed (unknowingly, or perhaps knowingly) toward my spiritual growth.

However difficult I found certain middle-to-later life experiences with my father, eventually, I better understood that one of his roles in my life was to be "seemingly" negative, as in my thirties asking if I needed a kick in the ass or in my early fifties telling me that I wasn't even a professional. At each of these and other times, I had lacked the emotional maturity to explain myself to him. That maturity wouldn't come until my late fifties.

Now, from my ability in my seventies to reflect, I understand that his deepest desire was to help me, but just possibly he found it hard to face that in some way he may have failed me—which wasn't true. Gratitude for my father, not for him as my father who was always there and which I had always felt, but for our difficulties, came in my mid-sixties with the healing of our relationship, as by then I'd matured through years of challenge into a woman who knew herself better and had proven herself.

My experiences with Jesse were different. I had maximum and transforming guidance from David, was more alert to opportunities in situations that arose between Jesse and me—and the changes we were making kept increasing, which I was aware of.

With Jesse, understanding and appreciation were closer to the moment and sufficient, due to my listening to David's spiritual viewpoints and my willingness to practice them. What was important was the new love growing in me. I was looking not for what I could receive, but for what I could give. When I felt pain from an old view being taken out, I affirmed I could and would change. Opposite but not contrary, when I looked at everything that *had* happened I affirmed that all had been necessary. Jesse and I were both in passage—in different ways—to a new kind of love.

CHAPTER 41

A Leap of Faith

2006–2007
2009–2019

How I remember my life is not the same
way someone else would have seen it....
Memories are tricky things. Everything we
experience is filtered through our mind,
and what comes out the other side has been
transformed.... That's the interesting thing
about books; they let you catch a glimpse
of the world through someone else's eyes."[1]

Ben Erickson

It was a dark morning at 5:30 on Meherabad Hill in 2005 when I was preparing to clean glass plaques while many others surrounded me, completing preparations for the largest pilgrim-attended three days of the year, Amartithi, the remembrance of Meher Baba dropping His physical form. As I looked around, an Indian man of medium build and height, his thick hair the color of snow at dusk and brushed back, and his eyes noticeably focused on me, approached and offered to help. I directed him toward Samadhi thinking he wanted to help clean the shrine, but he said no, that he wanted to help me. When I asked his name, he told me I could call him Old Man. Pausing, I said, "dear Old Man," and carrying my buckets and cloths, he followed me down the hill toward my other plaques, and in my silence began to talk. At the end of an hour, I turned to him saying, "You've been my father in many lifetimes." He smiled and replied that he'd been looking for me for three days. Later, at my home, when I handed him *A Flower for God*, he tapped the cover, and said, "This is about a leap of faith, and others will need to read it."

After Baba's message to stop writing, in February of 2004, the book had remained untouched for well over two years, until on a day of rain followed by a coral-orange sunset, the message came to return to writing.

I began waking up every night after twelve, knowing that I was to get up and write. At first I worked for two hours, then four and sometimes five. A few mornings, my day started at one-thirty because I never got back to bed. My first attempts brought frustration and left me overwhelmed. The original manuscript had spilled forth in enthusiasm. This time, I quickly realized, I had to teach myself how to organize writing.

I had changed the original title of *My Baba,* to a second try of

Reminiscence. Both were closed doors, and I remained standing outside, somehow dispassionate about the writing and therefore unable to get to it. Discouraged, I reacted by listing every word, phrase, and idea that came to mind for a title, until, by the twentieth attempt, my breathing quickened as I began to feel close. As I wrote *A Flower for God*, I felt the elation of its rightness. In Pat Schneider's words, "Experience has taught me to recognize the tiny jolt of joy that tells me a phrase or an image is worth pursuing."[2] And I had. The writing opened wide to my effort, and I knew how I was going to organize it.

Using a table, columns, and check marks, I chose what I wanted and made a rough draft. Calmed down by the structure, I began studying the story lines, the voice, sensory details, and the metaphors. As I rewrote, I saw a new kind of sentence appear that I recognized as previously beyond my ability. It was strong as bone and gave information partially viewed before in metaphor that now was clear, truthful, and accessible. When, in "The Hayloft," I wrote, "However not for forty-five years and in a place far from this one would I know of the unavoidable necessity and have the courage to face emotionally growing from a girl into a woman," I knew I was able to write deeper.

From November 2006 through January 2007, I had written at Meherabad then at the Florida farm, but by the end of January the writing was again stopped. I put the book away with no further thought of it for nearly three years—though I remembered the man who had seen a far broader reason for its purpose than I.

In December 2009, I began what I thought was a final draft to send to a friend who was both a published writer and an editor. I had known Anna Kirwan for twenty-nine years, but had not seen her for well over twenty, yet by our mutual feeling, an immediate bond renewed, and she agreed to be my editor. Throughout the month, I wrote and wrote in an effort to complete the entire book by my chosen date of January 10. During one writing session, I added up nineteen hours—but I soon discovered that my goal was unrealistic. However, by the following summer, after Anna read my draft, she called it a "spiritually intensely moving" memoir. I was thrilled.

From 2012 on, as Anna's health required a simpler life, I exchanged different final versions with my new editor Rosie Pearson. But with each version, I continued to remember more as I also discovered new writing ability. By November 2014, I understood that I had to change from the original topic format to a chronology—and this became the fourth, and awaited final draft. While reading Nora Roberts' *Stars*, I found a description of private investigator Cade Parris that partially reminded me of what I was doing: "Puzzles fascinated him. Locating pieces, shuffling them around, trying new angles until they slipped into place, was a challenge that had always satisfied him."[3] I was both writing and rewriting, for formerly separate parts were now joined.

Fourteen years after our first meeting, Dinesh Chibber, "dear Old Man," remains both a spiritual teacher and friend. Recently, I handed him a pre-publication draft of *A Flower for God,* as he had been asking if I had finished the book over the three past years. After reading several parts, he smiled—and then together we smiled.

Over the sixteen years of work on the book, the more difficult the writing situation became, the more I turned to Meher Baba for inspiration. "Honest and whole-hearted efforts will help you to find your personal path leading to Me"[4] was His encouraging message. Without His teachings, as the spiritual child David described at fifty-four, I could not have written *A Flower for God.*

LOVING

CHAPTER 42

Loved

1990S—2007

May 3 — early morning walk — heard the church bells —
a bobwhite — and saw an apple blossom — first one
I've seen. 6:30 A.M. — May 4th — heard the staccato of the
woodpecker this morning and saw the wake in the water
of the two ducks in the little pond as they swam around.

My mother

My geraniums on the windowsill have been superb. Lots
of large red blossoms. Have had good luck with cuttings
and creating new plants and making believe this is my
garden. Have a begonia that is in flower all the time.

Well, this is my first in a long time so attend it with grace.

New England love—Dad

These reminiscences recall moments from the last times I spent with each of my parents, but the word has a different meaning for each as I write about them. For my mother, I have drawn from the nine years before the ending of her life from Alzheimer's when she still lived at home in Rhode Island; living in Florida, I was too far away for more than annual visits. My memory begins one night at the Seraphim Center, the spiritual center where I had my counseling practice. At nine p.m., as I was locking the door to my office, I noticed a young client coming down the hall and thought that it was an unusual time for him to be there. When he stopped next to me I then thought that he wanted to make an appointment. Instead he said, "Your mother says, 'Thank you,'" paused long enough for me to thank him, and continued out of the building. I felt warmth from the pleasure of my mother's words. The next morning I received a call that her life had ended, and with the call I then understood the full significance of her last message to me the night before.

By the time of her service in May 2002 at the nursing home on Narragansett Bay where she had lived for eight years, I knew an inner freedom that allowed me to express my love for her in the way we had shared while she was still at home. On the last of my visits, before she stepped into a world of distance where moments gradually lessened in clarity, we would dance in the living room on the thick, soft, grayed-blue carpet, around a sunny yellow-covered chair (my dad liked Swedish colors) and by an antique-white sofa, under pastel paintings from their trip to Mykonos. Now when it was my turn to share at her service, I turned on a cassette of her favorite singer, Willie Nelson, and as if she were there in my arms, we danced as "On the Sunny Side of the Street" led us twirling around the lectern.

On the ride back to my older daughter's home, my son-in-law told me that he wasn't sure if people understood me, but that they had seen me as different from the person who they'd known. His thoughtful words pleased me—he'd recognized how clearly I had dared to express my heart.

By unusual circumstances, I saw my dad two months before the ending of his life, and later understood that we had been given a divine appointment. And so his is a lengthier memory.

From November to January was the wrong time to be traveling from India to my Florida home, since I would be going on to New England, which would require that I drive in winter conditions. But from a feeling I had, I thought that my dad might be approaching his final days, and I wanted to be with him. By this time, in 2006, he was in an assisted-living residence on a lake in northern Rhode Island near Cape Cod, where for years Paul, and I, and our young daughters had a weathered, gray-shingled cottage on a sand road. I missed the cottage, missed the scrub pines, missed South Village Beach, remembering being happy as a family. So I rented a heated cabin on the main street of Dennisport, and each morning I crossed the Sagamore Bridge onto the mainland of Massachusetts, then on to Rhode Island to visit my dad, returning in the late afternoon under a sky painted with warm reds and oranges.

On that first morning, standing in the doorway to his room, I saw him before he saw me. He was resting on his bed with the visor of his baseball hat sticking up like a duck's beak—"Cute," I'd thought. At his age-resistant, 6 foot 4¾ inch standing-tall height, he barely fit the bed's length. I spoke, and he turned his head. He was awake, and with recognition came a big smile of surprise, and, "Well, Prema."

"Hi, Dad." I felt so glad to be with him.

"Well, Prema," he repeated, "I see you've finally conquered India," as if he'd been holding those words for his first opportunity of seeing me. He spoke in his usual deep, resonant voice, and I could hear his satisfaction that I had finally found my place in the world, as he'd once said he couldn't die until I was taken care of.

"Well, Dad, I guess you could call it that." Unprepared for this compliment—and then suddenly realizing exactly what he had said, I became wordless. In that moment of his recognition and my astonishment, years of his challenging me disappeared.

Going to India alone for the first time in 1997, I had been misunderstood by my family as running away from responsibility. I was totally unfamiliar with Meher Baba, but between David's low-key suggestion that I might want to go to India and my tears upon first watching a video of Meher Baba, I had made my decision. As I kept returning to India, my dad began referring to jobs I could research. Each time that I told him I worked for God, his bewilderment was apparent. His glance would swing upward and aside. But, eventually I began to hear his pride in me, as when at the First Baptist Church in East Greenwich, he introduced me as "my daughter visiting from India."

I think it had been on that visit, or soon after, that he realized I could take care of myself, and this visit was his first opportunity to tell me. Once again he was the dad who had tossed the ball, the dad who had straightened my shoulders, who had given me all he had to give, the dad who loved me, and now, knowing that I had a place in the world, the dad who also knew that his work was finally done. I could feel his love beaming at me.

Experiencing the wonder of what had already happened, a totally unthought-of question popped out. "Dad, what do you think will happen when you physically die?" Not having prepared this, I was uncertain of what would happen now—a stilted silence? I waited, but he began to talk without hesitation. Hastily I looked at a bedside table and grabbed paper and a pen as he was saying that he'd been thinking about this, and I was rapidly writing what followed in an effort to get every word. He had obviously examined his beliefs, and although I kept all that he said, what follows is what had the most meaning for me.

My dad dealt with one big God of great intelligence and involved with all people, and he wanted to be a member of that God's Council, involved in its activities. When becoming cognizant of God, he hoped to be an assistant in whatever practical value that he had. What he did not want was to ache or hurt or have pain.

At this new residence, he would choose to be called by his given name of Wellington rather than Duke, which he'd gone by most of his life, and I think that he foresaw and was even already feeling a softening, a transformation, and a surrender, having finally achieved life's ultimate purpose—to know that he was eternal.

Walking with him to the dining room and glancing up, I noticed that he stood tall with acceptance and beneficence. While he maneuvered his walker, I paced my steps to its awkward gait, slowing to stay beside him, my pride of him coming in a rush. Then at his table, where two gentlemen and a lady were seated, he moved his walker aside and used the lady's to his left in what I realized was a ritual of cooperation at each meal. I fit in on his corner, and afterwards we returned to his room for the apple crisp (warmed for us) that I'd brought from Phantom Farm where he and my mother used to buy apples.

Standing by the swinging door, watching him leave in a van for a dental appointment, I felt sad that I couldn't join him, as if I was deserting him, but I knew that I needed to get over the canal before dark. It had already snowed one morning, proving that January was indeed a month recognized for its snowfalls.

In February, as his life was close to ending, I did not come from India as I both felt and knew that we had had our last visit. When his day did come, I took a garland of my love for him, my gratitude for his being my father, and of my celebration of him, and as I arrived on the hilltop I realized, "Oh, of course. It's Baba's birthday!" What a perfect day it was that I was bringing my dad's garland. His was going to be placed on the shrine on one of the most important days of the year. A bed of red roses, thousands of them, inches thick, covered the white marble, and on the porch, beautiful handmade decorations attached to its beams moved in the air creating a fluttering ceiling. After taking my garland in I found one seat left open and at that point heard what I thought was a familiar song. But how could it be? But yes, as I looked outside, a school band was marching up the hill playing John Philip Sousa's most famous march, "The Stars and Stripes Forever," one of my dad's favorite pieces of music. Believing in synchronicity, or that I had created a miracle, I held a smile, eyes wet, chin down then up, for my dad's soul was heading toward the light on Meher Baba's birthday and, in my heart, accompanied by his favorite march.

CHAPTER 43

Love

2015 CONTINUING
Love and happiness are the only
important things in life.... The
hidden depths of the ocean of life
can be gauged only by sounding
the heart.[1]

Meher Baba

I learned much from Jesse during the six early, fully-packed years of living at the farm—about Ayurvedic medicine, yoga, cooking sticky rice, buying a fresh apple, massage, reflexology—interspersed with his pointing out that if I wanted to help, I could clean, haul branches, or bump to "the Dixie" for coffee and half n' half. I listened to his prayers and poetry. When he built a meditation studio and a bedroom, I helped. I learned how to prune trees (then forgot), but I enjoyed doing all of it with him. He showed me that the sprinkler I'd put in the garden was watering the weeds, and I'd do better using the hose. I smiled. During a short time before bed, when a low lamp held us together from the end of the sofa where I sat to the chair where he tilted back, his feet on a corner of the table, he'd tell me simple information about history, or international news. Most important was what I listened to about Meher Baba, His writing, and, only slightly less so, other spiritual masters and their writing, holy women and their writing. In India, he took me to temples of Perfect Masters. He told me to walk behind him in the bazaar if I didn't know where I was going, and from that view, I learned how to take care of myself later, when I wanted to go on my own. It wasn't always direct teaching. I observed and learned as well.

I would not know if I was going back to the farm until a few weeks before leaving Meherabad. Accepting that Baba was in charge of all my life, I'd pack then wait. When I'd returned in 2006, my job had been to spar varnish the studio, finishing the remainder left after the three-quarters Jesse had done in September, when he'd also rebuilt the bathroom. Letting go of the intensity of living at Meherabad and in India in general, I moved to simple-minded time, watching the sun rise and set and the stars wink out, following the herds and flocks crossing from his woods to the neighbor's, looking at the variations of petal, leaf, bark, and branch of dogwood, redbud, cedar, hickory, southern pine, one magnolia, and whatever flowers and grasses wove the texture of the field.

Out early my first morning to tour the yard, taking in everything at once in the chill, I began at the kitchen windows, where a white jasmine I'd planted four years ago, protected from the cold on the south side, had sent vines to the roof and attached to screens. Gently I pulled them down, entwining them with lower branches on the narrow trellis neighbored between an old fig and a sego palm. When the north porch was rebuilt for a bedroom, the old jasmine (which had managed to regain some of its former glory), in the way of construction, had been removed. The future now belonged to this newer one, growing in profusion.

Jesse's farm would be sold in December 2015 following my last two weeks there that summer. My song "Red Bird" was written in an earlier year, and carried with it an undercurrent of a future leaving. Still I knew that in my heart, my love of these times and this place would live on.

RED BIRD *Song*

Red bird singing in a black fig tree,
Looking out my window what do I see?
Morning sun in a tangerine sky,
Red bird to a hickory tree will fly.

My home, my home,
Here for awhile 'til I leave to roam.
My home, in the greening green—
Grazing at sundown, deer come here.

Red bird singing in a loquat tree,
I'm just sitting in the quiet air.
Chair a'tilt and my feet up high,
Star-gazer looking at the moon so near.

My home, my home,
Here for awhile 'til I leave to roam.
My home, in the greening green
Red bird sighing in the trembling sky.

Red bird singing my song unseen.
My sweetheart's letter in my hand today.
Words I read made my heart change tune;
Two months more and we're together in June.

My home, my home,
Here for a rest from a working world.
My home, in the greening green
Red bird above me in a twilight sky.

PJC   2003

BECOMING

CHAPTER 44

My Journey Through a Spiritual Awakening with God

1990 CONTINUING

The whole idea is that you've got to
bring out again that which you went
to recover, the unrealized, unutilized
potential in yourself.[1]

Joseph Campbell

My parents married in 1941, settling near city relatives, until wanting to be independent they moved to the Bay Ridge area of Brooklyn on Colonial Road. By 1942 it was wartime and hanging laundry on the roof my mother could see black ships in the harbor. Pregnant with me, and claustrophobic, she was once on a subway during a blackout and must have felt terrified. She found my name on the society page for debutantes in a New York newspaper, and I was born Barbara Joan Cramer in February 1943. Always pronouncing my name as Bah bra, only when writing this chapter did I realize how much I had always liked hearing her say my name.

In my mid-forties, checking in for a flight and giving my name as Barbara Cramer, an agent asked me, "Which one are you?" I couldn't answer. What did she mean...which one am I? Due to my blank look, she asked me to step behind her counter where seeing her screen I immediately felt disconcerted. Forty entries of Barbara Cramer were in lists with a state below each. Searching, I found Massachusetts and still unable to speak, pointed.

At about fifty, I became increasingly disillusioned by my name having been that of a debutante's and began to think of what new interpretation it could have. Through Stephen I met Barbara Hero, and after listening to her experiments with sound in a pyramid in Egypt, I expressed my feelings about my name to her. From her knowledge, she then explained that Barbara means Ba Ba, twin souls, and Ra, the Sun God, giving me a new historical meaning for my first name. Next I remembered that Paul and I, in our second year of marriage, had driven through Domremy, France, the home of Joan of Arc, a Saint of courage, which now gave to Joan a different significance too.

At fifty-three, following the ending of Stephen's life, my new months alone blended from winter into spring, and I thought more and more of having a softer sounding name, one spiritual. The name Prema kept coming to me, but I was unsure that I was worthy of a name that meant divine love.

Then in June, as I was waiting to sign in at Amma's retreat, I felt a sudden knowing that I was Prema. And in spite of the resistance of the coordinator to accept my late entry, I prevailed. And then, Amma blessed it.

With Prema not yet on my passport, by the third week of the following January, with my first pilgrimage to Meherabad coming to an end, on my final visit to Baba's shrine, Baba let me know that I needn't bring a jasmine for I was His jasmine. And I became Prema Jasmine.

One day, when I felt drawn to look at the letters of my birth name, several of them dropped away. In Barbara, I now recognized Baba. In the fuller Barbara Joan, I saw Babajan, the Perfect Master of Poona. And I realized that in naming me as she did, my mother had planted the seeds of my spiritual journey.

SUPPLEMENT

I saw a door open[1]
Peter Schneider

AFTERWORD

May we open to a deeper understanding
and a genuine love and caring
for the multitude of faces
who are none other than ourself.[1]
Wendy Egyoku Nakao

From my years with Meher Baba, I know my inner self as quieter, and my outer self as more comfortable in the world. I smile and laugh more. I help others more. Feelings of separation have diminished and been replaced by my getting to know the real me. Through the situations Meher Baba has brought to help me grow, I've expanded in imagination and strengthened in courage and commitment. I live increasingly in kindness and gentleness, and most important—in constant gratitude. Happy, and happy for others, when failures do occur, I forgive myself, apologize, and look for a better way. I persevere and hold patience with a good grip on humor. My compass direction trues to uncovering the positive in everything. When I look at the big picture, I know guidance is there. When I look inward,

I know truth is there.

TouchStone   Process   June 29 – July 29, 1999

DE-CORDING

De-cording is a technique to eliminate harmful thoughts and emotions that prevent one from having a healthy relationship with the world. These emotions include fear, anger, jealousy, guilt, unworthiness, grief, loneliness, abandonment, and other negative thought forms and feelings. A de-cording session takes less than an hour and basically consists of a series of guided visualizations focusing on a particular person or situation that is problematic.

The word de-cording refers to the removal of attachments and connections, which are mental and psychic lines of energy that link every one of us to every person, place, concept, and even animal we have come in contact with. Cordings, both positive and negative, are constantly being created and destroyed and can accumulate from previous lifetimes. Many people are unaware of the existence of these bindings until they are brought to the surface of consciousness, through exposure by an adept and qualified energy worker. Successful de-cording does not require a belief in past lives or psychic ability but simply the intention to release painful thoughts and emotions and a willingness to quiet the mind and follow easy directions. Positive cordings hold thoughts and emotions that don't need to be managed or removed—for example gratitude, forgiveness, joy, contentment, cooperation, and others of this nature. These positive cordings are light and nourish a person's sense of self-reliance and personal satisfaction. Negative cordings restrict and inhibit one's ability to joyfully experience the present moment, curtailing the fullness of life. As unconscious thoughts and emotions are brought into the light of consciousness, they are then dissolved and eliminated by the de-cording method.

De-cording identifies damaging mental concepts and deep-seated emotions that with a minimum of discussion can be understood and corrected. By focusing on clearing out useless misconceptions, the mind and body become more relaxed and thus freer and better energized to use existing guidance, intuition, and love to rediscover the innate joy in life that comes with a clear and tranquil mind and heart. Emotional and mental clutter, although unconscious, can adversely affect the thoughts, feelings, and actions of our lives. Just as the garden grows better free of weeds and our homes provide greater harmony when pleasingly organized, so too does the mind respond to new knowledge and opening to the light of truth. De-cording is a simple, easy, and effective technique of freeing oneself from limitations connected with wrong thinking and inappropriate feelings. De-cording may be combined with intuitive counseling and healing work, depending on a person's needs or a particular situation.

The requisites for successful de-cording are the client's good intent, a safe environment, and the intuitive ability and experience of the practitioner. The cornerstone and guiding light of this transformative work is the expression and dissemination of Divine Love, which releases unlimited power for change.

AVATAR MEHER BABA

Compassionate Father

I HAVE COME

NOT TO TEACH

BUT TO AWAKEN.

Final passport on 21 August 1967

MEHER BABA 1894 – 1969

At nineteen, Merwan Sheriar Irani realized
His first unveiling as the Avatar of the Age.
Those Perfect Masters responsible were:
Hazrat Babajan of Poona, Narayan Maharaj
of Kedgaon, Tajuddin Baba of Nagpur, Sai
Baba of Shirdi, and Upasni Maharaj of Sakori.

At twenty-four, Merwan revealed Himself
to be a spiritual master. Within two years His
followers had recognized Him as Meher Baba.

Each year lovers, followers, and seekers
come to His Tomb-Shrine for Amartithi
to celebrate His dropping His body at noon
on January 31, 1969 under colorful pandals,
joined in a hush of silence for fifteen minutes.

PHOTOGRAPHS

The Second Writing Exercise
When everyone has settled down with writing
pad and pen after the first exercise, I ask the
group to remember a snapshot or a photograph
of someone close, a family member or a close
friend or lover. After a moment I ask them
to start writing with the words "In this one
you are..."[1]

Pat Schneider

THE HAYLOFT
The Farm, illustration by Paul Sherburne

THE HAYLOFT
Prema as a child on the farm

MARRIAGE AND CHILDREN
Prema and family

FIRST POETRY
Prema and Pat Schneider

BEGINNINGS AND ENDINGS
Prema at Beth's wedding

FINDING MY NICHE
Prema at Megan's wedding

DISCOVERING MY MOTHER
Rowena Cramer, Prema's mother

DISCOVERING MY FATHER
Wellington Cramer, Prema's father

LOVE, SERVE, FORGIVE
Stephen Michael Camp, Prema's second husband

LOVE, SERVE, FORGIVE
Prema on tour with Stephen

AUGUST
Lagoon Cabin

ADJUSTMENT
Prema at Meherabad

JESSE AND DAVID
Arnavaz Dadachanji
Photo by Prema

LOVE
Prema and Jesse

MY JOURNEY THROUGH A SPIRITUAL AWAKENING WITH GOD

Prema and her parents

NOTES

All quotes in this book cited from *A Course in Miracles* © are from the 3rd edition. Foundation for Inner Peace, P.O. Box 598, Mill Valley, CA 94942-0598. www.acim.org

THE HAYLOFT

1. Don Perkins, introduction to *The Barns of Maine: Our History, Our Stories* (Charleston, SC: The History Press, 2012), 11.

YARD AND HOME

1. *Discourses Vol. 1*, 4th ed. - Avatar Meher Baba Trust retrieve at https://www.avatarmeherbabatrust.org/Book_Files/Dis_5_V_Vi.pdf

GOSPEL TENTS AND THE UNITARIAN CHURCH

1. *Meher Baba Journal, Vol 1*, No. 12, (Meherabad, Ahmednagar, India: Meher Editorial Committee, October 1939) p. 1, lines 14 – 16. E-book retrieved at https://avatarmeherbabatrust.org/wp-content/uploads/2019/11/journal_1_12.pdf
2. Foundation for Inner Peace, *A Course in Miracles* ©, 3rd ed. (Mill Valley, CA: Foundation for Inner Peace, 2007) Lesson 171. https://acim.org/workbook/lesson-171/

3. Meher Baba, *Listen Humanity*, 3rd ed. (Atlanta, GA: Meherabad, 1985), 86. Ebook, 1955, Meherabad, LH 86, para. 35. Retrieve at: http://www.meherbabadnyana.net/life_eternal/Book_One/Death.htm

MARRIAGE AND CHILDREN

1. Elizabeth Roberts and Elias Amidon, eds., *Honoring the Earth: A Journal of New Earth Prayers* (New York, NY: HarperCollins Publishers, 1993), NP.
2. Paul Sherburne. Visit: paulsherburne.com
3. Meher Baba, *Silent Teachings of Meher Baba: Discourses and Conversations*, comp. and ed. Naosherwan Anzar (East Windsor, NJ: Beloved Archives, Inc., 2001), 156.
4. Carol McCabe, "Your Room is Booked," April 1, 2007. Retrieved at www.washingtonpost.com/wp-dyn/content/article/2007/03/30/AR2007033000818.html

FIRST POETRY

1. Pat Schneider, *Writing Alone and With Others* with a Foreword by Peter Elbow (New York: Oxford University Press, 2013), 240. In her book *How the Light Gets In: Writing as a Spiritual Practice*, Pat writes: "Peter Elbow is the informal 'dean' of the Writing Process Movement, a revolution in the teaching of creative writing in the United States that emerged in the 1970s." Visit www.patschneider.com, and for the writing method that she created, Amherst Writers & Artists (AWA), visit: www.amherstwriters.com
2. William Wordsworth and Samuel Taylor Coleridge, *Lyrical Ballads with a Few Other Poems,* 1798. See para. 26 at www.bartleby.com/39/36.html
3. Elizabeth McKim and Judith W. Steinbergh, *Beyond*

Words: Writing Poems with Children (Green Harbor, MA: Wampeter Press, 1983), 7.

4. Toi Derricotte, *The Empress of the Death House* (Detroit, MI: Lotus Press, 1978).

5. Pat Schneider, *How the Light Gets In: Writing as a Spiritual Practice* (New York: Oxford University Press, 2013), 177.

6. Kathryn J. Kvols and Bill Riedler, *Redirecting Children's Behavior: Workbook* (Seattle, WA: Parenting Press, 1998), 1–4.

7. Pat Schneider, *The Writer as an Artist: A New Approach to Writing Alone and with Others* (Los Angeles: Lowell House, 1994).

BEGINNINGS AND ENDINGS

1. Meher Baba, *Listen, Humanity*, 3rd ed. (Atlanta, GA: In Company with Meher Baba, 1985). Ebook, 104, para. 4. Retrieve at: https://www.avatarmeherbabatrust.org/Book_Files/ListenHumanity.pdf

VIOLIN, BALLET, ART

1. William Thetford. Visit: en.wikipedia.org/wiki/William_Thetford

2. William Thetford. Visit: en.wikipedia.org/wiki/William_Thetford

3. Helen Schucman. Visit: en.wikipedia.org/wiki/William_Thetford

4. Anna Kirwan–Vogel, *The Jewel of Life* (New York: Harcourt Brace Jovanovich, 1991).

FINDING MY NICHE

1. Lisa Schade Eckert, "The Jungian Self" in *How Does It Mean?* (Portsmouth, NH: Heinemann, (2006), 14.

2. Ira Progoff, *At A Journal Workshop* (New York: Dialogue

House Library, 1975). www.ableiam.com/progoff//writers.pdf

3. Schneider, *How the Light Gets In*, 24.
4. Christina Baldwin, *Life's Companion: Journal Writing as a Spiritual Quest* (New York: Bantam, 1991), 7.
5. Ani Tuzman. Visit: danceletters.com/about-ani
6. Margaret Robison, *The Long Journey Home: A Memoire* (New York: Spiegel & Grau, 2001). Mother of writers Augusten Burroughs and John Elder Robison.

DISCOVERING MY MOTHER

1. Meher Baba, *Silent Teachings*, 20.

DISCOVERING MY FATHER

1. Ben Erickson, *A Parting Gift* (New York: Warner Books, 2000), 269.
2. Wellington Cramer, "Staten Island Ferry-Boat." Read at: "Everyone is a Writer, Family Writing Part 6, 'A Raindrop Travelogue.'" www.purelyprema.com

ALWAYS LOVED

1. Stephen Michael Camp, "Barbara," personal collection. 1991.
2. Joseph Campbell, *The Hero's Journey: Joseph Campbell on His Life and His Collected Work,* ed. Phil Cousineau (Novato, CA: *New World Library,* 2003), 70–71.
3. Channeling by Barbara Cramer (Prema Camp) at Science of Mind, for a client, in St. Augustine, April 27, 1995.

EARLY OCCULT EXPERIENCES

1. Meher Baba, *Silent Teachings*, 77. Author's note: In our current language usage, both masculine and feminine

forms are used, which is different from the earlier period of Meher Baba when a masculine form was used to denote both men and women.

2. Maurice Sendak, *Where the Wild Things Are* (New York: Harper and Row, 1963; New York: Harper Collins, 2012), 3. Citation refers to Harper Collins edition.

3. Meher Baba, *Silent Teachings*, 79.

THE SEEDS OF INDIA

1. Perin Jasumani, *Gift of Love*, comp. (Pune, India: Meher Era Publication, 2000), 24.

LIVING IN THE PRESENT

1. Henry Wadsworth Longfellow, "The Psalm of Life," *Voices of the Night*, 1st ed., 1839. Read at: /www.poetryfoundation.org/poems/44644/a-psalm-of-life

2. For more information about the Lambdoma Keyboard, visit www.lambdoma.com

3. Foster Perry, *When Lightning Strikes a Hummingbird: The Awakening of a Healer* (Rochester, VT: Bear & Company, 1993).

4. Lawrence Furman, *Memoir of a Slightly Mad Mystic: How Dying Saved My Life* (Novato, CA: Inner Voice Press, 2017).

5. Meher Baba, *God Speaks* (Oakland, CA: Dharma Enterprises, 1955), Overleaf, para 1.

6. Stephen Michael Camp, "You Can't Go Back," *Surrender* (Amherst, MA: Watercourse Studios, 1992), Cassette.

7. Meher Baba, *The Everything and the Nothing* (Beacon Hill, Australia: Meher House Publications, 1963), 62.

LOVE, SERVE, FORGIVE

1. Stephen Michael Camp, "Sweet Surrender," *Surrender*

(Amherst, MA: Watercourse Studios, 1992), Cassette.

2. Edwene Gaines, *The Four Spiritual Laws of Prosperity: A Simple Guide to Unlimited Abundance* (New York: Rodale Books, 2005).

3. For more information about Joy Gardner, visit: highvibrations.net/

4. Jonathan Goldman, *Healing Sounds: The Power of Harmonics* (Rochester, VT: Healing Arts Press, 2002).

5. For more information about Jonathan Goldman, read the Robert Mann interview at: healingsounds.com/healing-sounds

6. Stephen Michael Camp, "Teach Only Love," *Surrender* (Amherst, MA: Watercourse Studios, 1992), Cassette.

7. Pete A. Sanders Jr., *You are Psychic: The Free Soul Method* (Flagstaff, AZ: Light Technology, 1989). Visit: www.freesoul.net

8. For more information about Sathya Sai Baba, visit: sathyasai.org/

9. Stephen Michael Camp, "Embodiment of Love (*Prema Swarupa*)," *Watermelon Seeds* (Gainesville, FL Mirror Image Studios, 1996), Cassette.

10. For more information about Mātā Amritānandamayī Devī, also known as Amma, visit: www.amma.org

THINK LOVE

1. Stephen Michael Camp, "Think Love," *Surrender* (Amherst, MA: Watercourse Studios, 1992), Cassette.

2. Paul Ferrini, *Love Without Conditions* (Greenfield, MA: Heartways Press, 1994). Visit: www.lightforthesoul.com/home

3. Stephen Michael Camp, "Good-Bye to New England," (Springfield, MA: 1993), Video.

4. Stephen Michael Camp, "Sail With Me," *Watermelon Seeds* (Gainesville, FL: Mirror Image Studios, 1996), Cassette.

5. Dr. Jon Mundy, *A Course in Mysticism and Miracles: Begin*

Your Spiritual Adventure (Newburyport, MA: Red Wheel/ Weiser/Conari, 2018). Visit: www.drjonmundy.com/

6.   Linda Camp (Linda C. Chrystal) and Stephen Camp, (Stephen Michael Camp), "I Am a Shepherd's Child," *Coming Home* (Albuquerque, NM: Holy Smoke Studios, © Linda Camp, Inspirational poem; © Stephen Camp, arr. lyrics music, 1986), Cassette.

7.   Camp, *Surrender.*

8.   Paul Ferrini, *Crossing the Water: A Poetic Exploration of Healing and Forgiveness in Our Relationships* (Greenfield, MA: Heartways Press, 1997), 79–80. Chapter quote by permission of Paul Ferrini.

9.   Stephen Michael Camp, "I Find Peace" (Multilingual), *Watermelon Seeds* (Gainesville, FL: Mirror Image Studios, 1996), Cassette.

10. Caroline Myss (pronounced *mace*). Visit: www.myss.com/ about-caroline-myss/

11. Camp, "I Find Peace."

12. Ferrini, *Love Without Conditions,* chap. 4%, Kindle.

13. Meher Baba, *God Speaks*, 190.

APRIL TO MAY

1.   Bal Natu, *Glimpses of the God Man*, Vol. 6 (North Myrtle Beach: Sheriar Foundation, 1997), 92.

2.   David Cousins, *A Handbook for Light Workers,* ed. Jean Prince (Bath, UK: Barton House, 1993).

3.   For more information about lightworkers, visit: https:// www.happiness.com/en/magazine/inspiration-spirituality/ what-is-a-lightworker-and-what-do-they-do-exactly/

4.   Jamie Sams and David Carson, *Medicine Cards, The Discovery of Power Through the Ways of Animals* (New York: St. Martin's Press, 1988).

JUNE TO JULY

1. Daniel Goleman, *Emotional Intelligence: Why It Can Matter More Than IQ* (New York: Bantam, 1995), 46.

2. Meher Baba, *Letters from the Mandali of Avatar Meher Baba*, Vol. II, comp. and ed. Jim Mistry (North Myrtle Beach, SC: Sheriar Press, Inc., 1983), 110–111.

AUGUST

1. Meher Spiritual Center, Pamphlet. See: www.mehercenter.org

SEPTEMBER TO OCTOBER

1. Bal Natu, *Showers of Grace*, comp. Bal Natu (Hyderabad, India: Avatar Meher Baba Andhra Centre, 1984), para. 3. www.ambhc.org/baba_bal8.html

LIVING ALONE AND YET TOGETHER

1. Meher Baba, *Sparks from Meher Baba*, 2nd ed. comp. by Delia de Leon and Kitty Davy (Ahmednagar, IN: Avatar Meher Baba Trust eBook, 2011), p. 17, para. 5. Retrieve at: https://avatarmeherbabatrust.org/wp-content/uploads/2019/11/Sparks-from-Meher-Baba.pdf

A PILGRIMAGE

1. Meher Baba, *Meher Baba Calling,* 6th ed., (Ahmednagar, India: Meher Nazar Books, 1992), 12.

ADJUSTMENT

1. Mani S. Irani, *82 Family Letters to the Western Family of Lovers and Followers of Meher Baba* (North Myrtle Beach,

SC: Sheriar Foundation, 1976), 176.

A NEW AND DIFFERENT LIFE

1.　Meher Baba, *Silent Teachings*, 114.
2.　Ira G. Dietrick, *The Mastery of Consciousness: An Introduction and Guide to Practical Mysticism and Methods of Spiritual Development as Given by Meher Baba*, comp. and ed. Allan Y. Cohen, reprinted by permission of Ira G. Dietrick (New York: Harper Colophon, 1977), 117–118.

A MINISTRY OF COUNSELING

1.　C. B. Purdom, *The God–Man: The Life, Journeys and Work of Meher Baba with an Interpretation of his Silence and Spiritual Teaching* (North Myrtle Beach, SC: Sheriar Foundation, 1964), 296.
2.　Jesse Massa, "Decording," *TouchStone*, June 29–July 29, 1999, 14. A discontinued spiritual information newspaper. See Supplement for excerpted article published with permission by the author, 346–347.
3.　Jai Josefs, "I Love Myself the Way I Am." Listen at: www.youtube.com/watch?v=HjVveBDn5Kc
4.　For more information about Meredith Moon, visit: https://meredithmoonphd.com/about-me

TRUE SELF: INNER CHILD — INNER PARENT

1.　Lucia Capacchione, *Recovery of Your Inner Child, The Highly Acclaimed Method for Liberating Your Inner Self* (New York: Simon & Schuster/Fireside, 1991).
2.　Margaret Robison, *The Long Journey Home: A Memoir* (New York: Spiegel & Grau, 2001).
3.　Jai Josefs, "I Love Myself the Way I Am." Listen at:

www.youtube.com/watch?v=HjVveBDn5Kc

JESUS

1. To hear singer Cat Stevens' rendition of the 1931 hymn, "Morning Has Broken," listen at: www.youtube.com/watch?v=eoTInLOJuUM
2. Stephen Michael Camp, "Think Love," *Surrender* (Amherst, MA: Watercourse Studios, 1992), Cassette.
3. Ibid, "Give Him Your Hand."

"BABA"

1. Meher Baba, *Beams from Meher Baba on the Spiritual Panorama* (Perennial Library), ed. C. D. Deshmukh (New York: Harper & Row, 1971), 39–41.
2. Meher Baba, *Discourses*, 7th rev. ed. (Myrtle Beach, SC: Sheriar Foundation, 1987), xiii.
3. Arnavaz N. Dadachanji, *Gift of God* (East Windsor, NJ: Naosherwan Anzar Beloved Books, 1996), vi.

GOD-GIVEN GIFTS

1. Meher Baba, *Meher Baba Calling,* 20.
2. For more information about Andrew Harvey, visit: andrewharvey.net
3. 5 Reasons Why You Are Seeing 11:11 – The Meaning of 1111... Retrieved at https://willowsoul.com/blogs/numbers/5-reasons-why-you-are-seeing-11-11-the-meaning-of-1111
4. Robert L. Camp, *Love Cards: What Your Birthday Reveals about You and Your Personal Relationships* (Naperville, IL: Sourcebooks, 1997).

A BETTER WAY

1.   Meher Baba, *Life At Its Best*, ed. Ivy O. Duce (San Francis-
     co, CA: Sufism Reoriented, Inc., 1957), 43.
2.   Campbell, *The Hero's Journey*, 52.
3.   Ibid.

THE HILL IN SEPTEMBER

1.   Mehera J. Irani, *Mehera,* comp. and ed. Janet Judson with
     Shelley Marrich (East Windsor, NJ: Naosherwan Anzar
     Beloved Books, 1989), 109.

MESSAGE IN SAMADHI

1.   Meher Baba, *The Silent Master, Meher Baba*, comp. Irwin Luck
     (Myrtle Beach, SC: Meher Baba Archives Publishing, 1987), 179.

MY ROOM

1.   Mehera J. Irani, *Baba Loved Us Too*: *Stories of Baba and
     His Pets* (North Myrtle Beach, SC: Sheriar Books), 1–2.

WRITE DEEPER

1.   Pat Schneider, *How the Light Gets In*, 228.
2.   Amiya Kumar Hazra, *The Memoirs of a Zetetic: My Life
     with Meher Baba* (Hyderabad, India: Meher Mownavani
     Publications, 2001).

LOVE ALONE PREVAILS

1.   Delia DeLeon, *The Ocean of Love* (North Myrtle Beach,
     SC: Sheriar Foundation, 1991), 85. Arlene Stearns, *Living
     with Meher Baba*, para. 1. Retrieved at: http://www.

mischievouspeeps.com/books/living-with-meher-baba/

2. Kitty Davy, *Love Alone Prevails* (North Myrtle Beach, SC: Sheriar Foundation, 2001).

JESSE AND DAVID

1. Meher Baba, *Life at Its Best*, ed. Ivy O. Duce (San Francisco, CA: Sufism Reoriented Inc., 1957), 23. Retrieve at: https://ambppct.org/Book_Files/Life.pdf

2. Meher Baba, *Beams from Meher Baba on the Spiritual Panorama*, 62–54.

ON MY OWN

1. Rano Gayley, *Because of Love: My Life and Art with Meher Baba*, ed. Ann Conlon (North Myrtle Beach, SC: Sheriar Press, 1983), 31.

WEST AND EAST

1. Meher Baba, *Silent Teachings*, 114.

MY SCOOTER

1. Eruch Jessawala, *Is That So?*, comp. Bill Le Page (Ahmednagar, India: Meher Nazar Books, 1985), 83.

TRIALS

1. Meher Baba, *God Speaks,* 2nd ed., rev. and enlarged (Walnut Creek, CA: Sufism Reoriented, 1973), 190.

A LEAP OF FAITH

1. Ben Erickson, *A Parting Gift* (New York: Warner Books,

2000), 27.

2. Nora Roberts, *Hidden Star (Stars of Mithra)* (Rockland, MA: Wheeler Publishing, Inc., 2008).

3. Schneider, *How the Light Gets In*, 13.

4. Bal Natu, *Glimpses of the God-Man, Meher Baba*, Vol. 6 (North Myrtle Beach, SC: Sheriar Foundation, 1984), 196.

LOVE

1. Meher Baba, *Discourses*, 97.

MY JOURNEY THROUGH A SPIRITUAL AWAKENING WITH GOD

1. Campbell, *The Hero's Journey*, 223.

SUPPLEMENT

1. Peter Schneider, *Line Fence* (Amherst, MA: Amherst Writers & Artists Press, 2006), 3.

AFTERWORD

1. Roberts and Amidon, *Honoring the Earth*, NP.

PHOTOGRAPHS

1. Schneider, *The Writer as an Artist*, 175.

ABOUT THE AUTHOR

1. Baldwin, *Life's Companion*, 7.

PUBLICATIONS

POETRY, SONG, RECORDING, &
ILLUSTRATION APPEARING IN THIS BOOK

PUBLISHED POETRY

As Barbara Sherburne (Prema Jasmine Camp)

"Gladys Buswell Titcomb": *Peregrine Vol. 2*, 1984.
"Bar Harbor": *Peregrine Vol. 1*, 1983.
"The Gift": *mother's manual*, 1975.
"I Love You": *mother's manual*, 1975.
"Monet's Water Lilies": *The Christian Science Monitor*,
September 1985.
"My Father's Tomatoes": *Peregrine Vol. 3*, 1985.
"When We Met": *Peregrine Vol. IV*, No. 1, 1986.

As Barbara Cramer (Prema Jasmine Camp)

"Canasta": *My Father's Tomatoes Chapbook 1*, 1993.
"Ripening": *The New York Quarterly*, 1993.
"The Way the Day Begins": *The Bellingham Review*, Vol. 18,
No. 2 (Issue 38), Fall 1995.
"Flowers": *My Father's Tomatoes Chapbook 1*, 1993.
"Acadia": *My Father's Tomatoes Chapbook 1*, 1993.
"Orange *One*, Orange *Two*": *My Father's Tomatoes Chapbook 1*,
1993.

UNPUBLISHED POETRY

As Prema Jasmine Camp

"Amid chatter"
"August"
"Wind"
"Harry's Apples"
"To An Angry Daughter"
"Beyond Reach"
"Facing Early Alzheimer's"
"Robert Cootey"
"Here"
"Santa Fe Wedding Dress"
"Willing"
"Perhaps"
"Peach Orchard"

By Wellington Cramer

"Staten Island Ferry-Boat"

PUBLISHED SONGS

As Barbara Joan Camp (Prema Jasmine Camp)

"River of Light," *Watermelon Seeds,* Stephen Michael Camp
(Gainesville, FL: Mirror Image Studios, 1996), Cassette.

UNPUBLISHED SONGS

As Prema Jasmine Camp

"Merry-Go-Round"
"Awaken"
"God is Good"

"Heart of God"
"Healing"
"Red Bird"

PUBLISHED ALBUMS

As Linda Camp (Linda C. Chrystal) and
Stephen Camp (Stephen Michael Camp)

"I Am a Shepherd's Child," *Coming Home* (Albuquerque, NM:
Holy Smoke Studios, © Linda Camp, Inspirational poem;
© Stephen Camp, arr. lyrics music, 1986), Cassette.

As Stephen M. L. Camp (Stephen Michael Camp)

Surrender (Amherst, MA: Watercourse Studios, 1992), Cassette.

As Stephen Michael Camp

Watermelon Seeds (Gainesville, FL Mirror Image Studios, 1996),
Cassette.

PUBLISHED ILLUSTRATION

Paul Sherburne, ink sketch of L. W. Titcomb Farm, North
Newport, Maine (*My Father's Tomatoes Chapbook 1*, 1993).

PEOPLE REFERRED TO IN THIS BOOK

Adi Dubash. A close one of Meher Baba (one who had the special privilege of always having access to Meher Baba) and was a former Trustee of the Avatar Meher Baba Perpetual Public Charitable Trust.

Buddha. According to Meher Baba, Buddha was the fourth of seven Avatars, following Krishna. "Buddha postulated the Four Noble Truths and the Eightfold Path." James H. McGrew, *Avataric Advents*, 2nd ed. (n.d.: The Beguine Library, 2010), 15. (Author's note: Using words from McGrew's book seemed the most accurate and consistent approach for explaining the seven Avatars. His name spellings are different. I've used the commonly found spellings.

Colonel Dinesh Chibber, Ret. Spiritual teacher.

Gurumayi. Gurumayi Chidvilasananda is the current spiritual head of the Siddha Yoga path.

Gyüto Tantric Monks. Monks who fled to India after a 1950 Chinese invasion of Tibet. In 1995, they travelled to the United States to perform as the "Gyüto Monks Tantric Choir."

Hazrat Babajan. A perfect master.

Helen Steiner Rice. An American writer of religious and inspirational poetry.

Jesus. According to Meher Baba, Jesus was the fifth of seven avatars following Buddha. "Meher Baba paints an entirely different picture of Jesus from the serious and humorless figure who often emerges from the Christian tradition. The real Jesus was full of Avataric humor, light-hearted about everything but God, magnetic, and a Master in every sense of the word." James H. McGrew, *Avataric Advents*, 141.

Krishna. According to Meher Baba, Krishna was the third Avatar following Ram. "There is a special aura of joy and sweetness attached to Krishna.... Krishna blessed the world with His love and merriment, and to this day paintings or statues of Krishna carry the fragrance of that love." McGrew, *Avataric Advents*, 225.

Lawrence Furman. A trance medium and author of *Memoir of a Slightly Mad Mystic: How Dying Saved My Life* that details his three near-death experiences and their impact in his life.

Meerama (Mother Meera). A holy woman, born in India, whose followers believe to be the incarnation of the Divine Mother.

Mehera Jehangir Irani. Meher Baba's closest mandali. Meher Baba called her "the purest soul in the universe."

Muhammad. According to Meher Baba, Muhammad was the sixth Avatar following Jesus. "Meher Baba revealed that Muhammad was an Avatar even though Muhammad Himself took pains to disclaim such status.... This man of humble origins inspired one of the world's major religions which now has over one billion adherents." McGrew, *Avataric Advents*, 109.

Narayan Maharaj. A perfect master.

Patrick Lyndon Nugent. The son of Patrick John Nugent and Luci Baines Johnson, and grandson of former U.S. President Lyndon B. Johnson.

Ram. Ram. According to Meher Baba, Ram was the second Avatar following Zoroaster. "One of the most famous devotees of Rama in the past century was Mahatma Gandhi, who as a devoted Hindu took Rama as the Avatar. [Gandhi's] last words, uttered as he was assassinated in 1948, are inscribed on his memorial: 'O Ram!'" McGrew, *Avataric Advents*, 275.

Rev. Carlos W. Anderson. An inspirational and transformational minister, composer, and recording artist as well as author.

Rev. Dr. Diane Berke. Founder and Spiritual Director of One Spirit Learning Alliance and One Spirit Interfaith Seminary in New York City.

Rev. Dr. Robert Estling. Co-founder with his wife, Rev. Dr. Janet Claire Moore, of Seraphim Center.

Sai Baba of Shirdi. A perfect master.

Sathya Sai Baba. An Indian guru, spiritual leader, and philanthropist.

Shadrach, Meshach, Abednago. Three Hebrew men written of in the Old Testament in the Book of Daniel who survived being thrown in a furnace through Divine intervention.

Tajuddin Baba. A perfect master.

Thomas Wolfe. "Tom Wolfe," 1931–2018. A journalist and best-selling author known for the New Journalism, using fiction-writing techniques in journalism.

Upasni Maharaj. A perfect master.

Zoroaster (Also Zarathustra). According to Meher Baba, the earliest Avatar. "Thousands of years ago, he [Zarathustra] gave to the world the essence of Truth in the form of three fundamental precepts–Good Thoughts, Good Words, and Good Deeds." Meher Baba as quoted in McGrew, *Avataric Advents*, 279.

GLOSSARY

Alliance of Divine Love. An international interfaith ministry founded by Rev. Dr. Barbara Selwa in 1971.

Amartithi. The Eternal Date, the anniversary of the day when Avatar Meher Baba dropped his physical form, is commemorated in a major gathering attended by thousands of visitors to Meherabad from January 30 to February 1 each year. During this 48-hour period a program of song, dance, and film continues all day and through much of the night on the stage near Meher Baba's Tomb. The climax of the event takes place on Amartithi day itself when, for fifteen minutes, the assembled crowd keeps silent in honor of the physical passing of the Avatar of the Age at 12:15 p.m. on January 31, 1969. The town of Meherabad hosts 10,000–12,000 overnight visitors and 25,000–30,000 daytime visitors from all over the world during a three-day program in celebration of Amartithi. Many of Meher Baba's followers celebrate Amartithi outside of India, mainly in Australia, Europe, and the United States. http://trustmeher.org/%20meher-baba-events/amartithi

Ashram. A religious retreat.

Avatar. "The total manifestation of God in human form on earth, as the Eternal Living Perfect Master;" Meher Baba, *Discourses*, 7th rev. ed., eds. Eruch B. Jessawala, J. Flagg Kris, and Bal Natu (Myrtle Beach, SC: Sheriar Press, 1987), 410.

Beguine. A dance of West Indian origin.

Blue bus. This bus was the vehicle that Meher Baba travelled on in 1938 throughout South India, accompanied by Eastern and Western women mandali.

Bread Loaf. A Writers' Conference founded in 1926 by *The New Yorker* magazine and held every summer in Middlebury, Vermont.

Coptic. The Christian Coptic Church of Egypt whose diaspora includes Americans of Coptic descent.

Darshan. "[T]he act of seeing; folding of hands in adoration or bowing at the feet to express devotion to the one worshiped." Meher Baba, *Discourses,* 411.

Ghats. Two mountain ranges in central and southern India. The Western Ghat is mentioned in the book.

Jai Baba. Victory to Baba, or Hail Baba. The customary greeting among Baba devotees.

Jain. An ancient Indian religion.

Karma. "The natural and necessary happenings in one's life, preconditioned by one's past lives." Meher Baba, *Discourses,* 412.

Lightworker. One who aims to bring love and light into this world by healing themselves and sharing their inner gifts with the world.

Mandali. The inner circle of disciples of Meher Baba.

Meherabad. The site of Avatar Meher Baba's Tomb-Shrine (Samadhi) and site of world pilgrimage. His early primary residence, ashram, and headquarters of His activities until 1944.

Meherazad. Meher Baba's personal residence for the second part of His advent now a primary site of world pilgrimage to Avatar Meher Baba in India.

"Morning Has Broken." A well-known Christian hymn first published in 1931. Words by English author Eleanor Fargeon.

National Collection of Fine Arts. Originally named The Smithsonian Art Collection when the early collection was first displayed in 1829 in various Smithsonian buildings, it is now called The Smithsonian American Art Museum and is located in the Old Patent Office in Washington, DC.

National Poetry Foundation (NPF). Established in 1971 at the University of Maine to foster the study of modern and contemporary poetry. The NPF sponsors conferences for scholars and writers and is internationally recognized.

Om Sai Ram. A spiritual mantra with a holy sound and the holy names of Perfect Master Sai Baba of Shirdi and Ram.

Perfect Master. "A God-Realized soul who retains God-consciousness and creation-consciousness simultaneously, and who works in creation to help other souls toward the Realization of God." Meher Baba, *Discourses*, 416.

Pilgrim Retreat. (Meher Pilgrim Retreat). A retreat center located in Meherabad, the ashram established by Meher Baba in 1923 near the town of Ahmadnagar in India. The center accommodates short-term stays for pilgrims who want to learn more about Meher Baba.

Sanskaras. "Impressions; accumulated imprints of past experiences, which determine one's desires and actions." Meher Baba, *Discourses*, 417.

Seraphim Center. An interfaith spiritual center, dedicated to the Light, located in Gainesville, Forida.

Shariat. The outward forms of religion.

Wounded Knee. A massacre of Native Americans by U.S. soldiers in 1890 in the area of Wounded Knee Creek in South Dakota.

Zetetic. A seeker, a doubter.

ABOUT THE AUTHOR

Writing makes a map, and there is
something about a journey that begs
to have its passage marked.[1]

Prema Jasmine Camp resides in India at Meherabad, the site of Samadhi, the Tomb-Shrine of Avatar Meher Baba, and a destination of world pilgrimage. Here she writes her blog, *Purely Prema*, for a global audience and has served the community in various capacities over the past sixteen years. In her earlier years, Prema toured the East Coast, the South, the Southwest, and California with Stephen Michael Camp, sound healer, musician, and later her husband. Stephen presented the healing vibrations of his music. Prema offered writing workshops, and both gave intuitive readings. Following his passing, she became an Alliance of Divine Love minister and an Emotional Health intuitive counselor at an interfaith spiritual center in Florida before her move to India. An early member of the international writers' organization Amherst Writers & Artists, Prema became a certified facilitator that led to the founding of her own writing community and now this first book, a deeply inspiring memoir of her spiritual awakening.

Made in the USA
Coppell, TX
20 October 2022

84997790R00226